# SUMMER FUN JUMBLE®

*Lazy Day*

## WORD PLAY

### by Henri Arnold, Bob Lee, and Mike Argirion

**TRIUMPH**
BOOKS
CHICAGO

This book is available at special discounts
for your group or organization.

For further information, contact:

Triumph Books LLC
814 North Franklin Street
Chicago, IL 60610
(800) 888-4741
(312) 337-1807 FAX

ISBN: 978-1-57243-114-0

Printed in the USA

# CONTENTS

## CLASSIC

### Summer Fun Jumble #1 – #32

## DAILY

### Summer Fun Jumble #33 – #167

## CHALLENGER

### Summer Fun Jumble #168 – #180

## ANSWERS

# CLASSIC

## SUMMER FUN
### JUMBLE®

# JUMBLE®

Unscramble these four Jumbles,
one letter to each square, to
form four ordinary words.

**RODLE**

**DAHEA**

**BEHREY**

**LUNYUR**

STILL a knockout, at her age!

WHAT THEY SAID WHEN
VENUS OF MILO
CAME TO DINNER.

Now arrange the circled letters
to form the surprise answer, as
suggested by the above cartoon.

ANSWER here ⬜⬜⬜⬜ **GOTTA** ⬜⬜⬜⬜⬜ **IT TO** ⬜⬜⬜⬜!

2

# JUMBLE®

Unscramble these four Jumbles,
one letter to each square, to
form four ordinary words.

**AZIME**

**NOSOW**

**TOLBET**

**PERRAY**

WHAT THEY MIGHT
HAVE AT AN
ITALIAN PICNIC.

Now arrange the circled letters
to form the surprise answer, as
suggested by the above cartoon.

Print the SURPRISE ANSWER here " ◯◯◯◯ – ◯◯◯◯ "

3

# JUMBLE®

Unscramble these four Jumbles, one letter to each square, to form four ordinary words.

NAIGG

NAHCT

STEWEN

ZACMEE

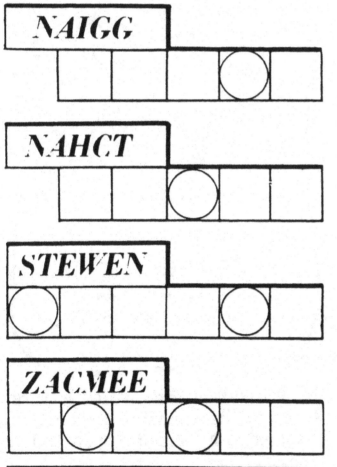

This is the place

WHERE YOU MIGHT FIND GOOD FRENCH SOUP?

Now arrange the circled letters to form the surprise answer, as suggested by the above cartoon.

Print the SURPRISE ANSWER here

IN "⬡⬡⬡⬡⬡⬡"

# JUMBLE®

Unscramble these four Jumbles, one letter to each square, to form four ordinary words.

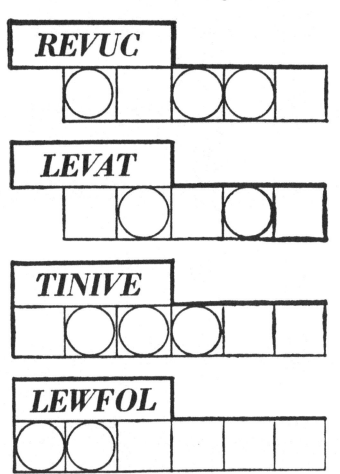

REVUC

LEVAT

TINIVE

LEWFOL

Wonderful country

FRENCH TOAST.

Now arrange the circled letters to form the surprise answer, as suggested by the above cartoon.

Print the SURPRISE ANSWER here

LA

▲▽▲▽▲▽▲▽▲▽▲▽▲▽▲▽▲▽▲▽▲▽▲▽▲▽

# JUMBLE®

Unscramble these four Jumbles, one letter to each square, to form four ordinary words.

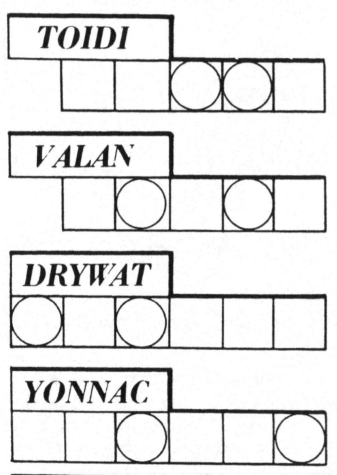

**TOIDI**

**VALAN**

**DRYWAT**

**YONNAC**

Print the SURPRISE ANSWER here

Chop! Chop!

WHAT A THIRSTY MAN MIGHT DO IN FORMOSA.

Now arrange the circled letters to form the surprise answer, as suggested by the above cartoon.

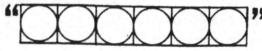 " ⬡⬡⬡⬡⬡⬡⬡ "  ⬡⬡

# JUMBLE®

Unscramble these four Jumbles,
one letter to each square, to
form four ordinary words.

**TILMI**

**USCOT**

**DEKBEC**

**EDGERD**

Print the SURPRISE ANSWER here

'Hmph! My
son, the
mower!

WHY YOU SHOULD
NEVER LET GRASS
GROW UNDER
YOUR FEET.

Now arrange the circled letters
to form the surprise answer, as
suggested by the above cartoon.

IT

# JUMBLE®

Unscramble these four Jumbles, one letter to each square, to form four ordinary words.

POLEE

BRIHC

NUCHAH

INDAGE

FRUIT SOMETIMES FOUND IN THE SAND.

Now arrange the circled letters to form the surprise answer, as suggested by the above cartoon.

Print the SURPRISE ANSWER here A

8

# JUMBLE®

Unscramble these four Jumbles,
one letter to each square, to
form four ordinary words.

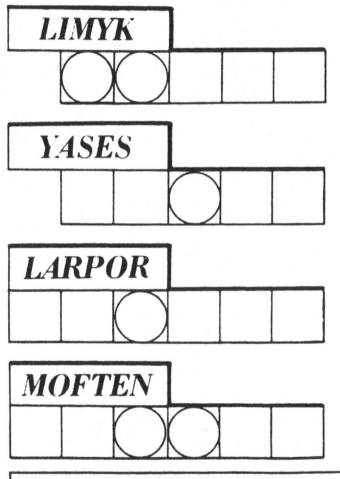

**LIMYK**

**YASES**

**LARPOR**

**MOFTEN**

WHAT PEOPLE WHO DON'T SUMMER IN THE COUNTRY OFTEN DO IN THE CITY.

Now arrange the circled letters
to form the surprise answer, as
suggested by the above cartoon.

Print the SURPRISE ANSWER here

9

# JUMBLE®

Unscramble these four Jumbles,
one letter to each square, to
form four ordinary words.

TEJEC

HABIS

RELILK

BONGLE

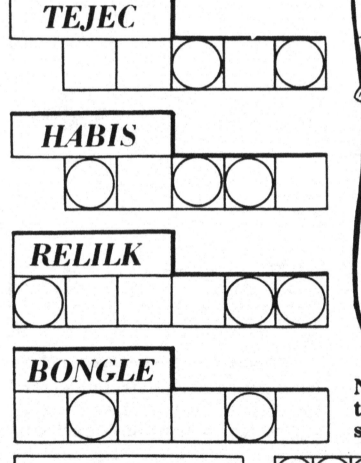

SOME VETERAN
GARDENERS MIGHT FIND
THIS THE HARDEST
THING TO RAISE.

Now arrange the circled letters
to form the surprise answer, as
suggested by the above cartoon.

Print the SURPRISE ANSWER here

# JUMBLE®

Unscramble these four Jumbles,
one letter to each square, to
form four ordinary words.

**LAMDY**

**EXIDO**

**YURKET**

**DIBOLE**

Print the SURPRISE ANSWER here

How'll
we get
home?

RACING

BURP!

A TEN-LETTER WORD THAT
STARTS WITH G-A-S.

Now arrange the circled letters
to form the surprise answer, as
suggested by the above cartoon.

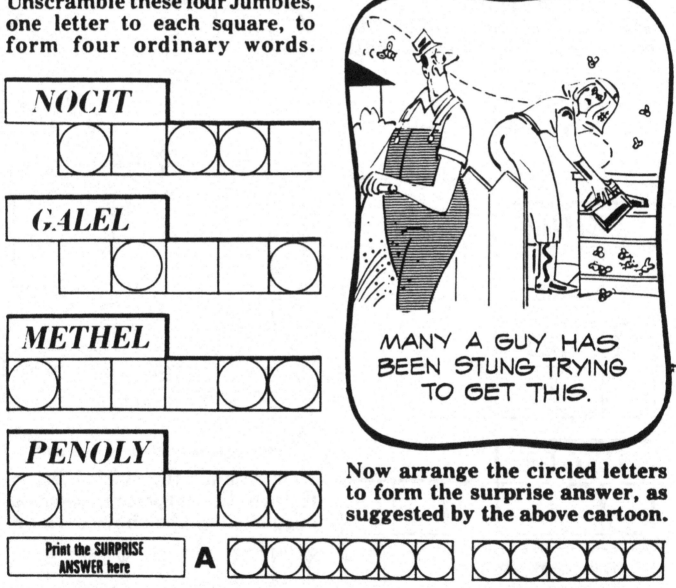

# JUMBLE®

Unscramble these four Jumbles, one letter to each square, to form four ordinary words.

**NOCIT**

**GALEL**

**METHEL**

**PENOLY**

MANY A GUY HAS BEEN STUNG TRYING TO GET THIS.

Now arrange the circled letters to form the surprise answer, as suggested by the above cartoon.

Print the SURPRISE ANSWER here

A

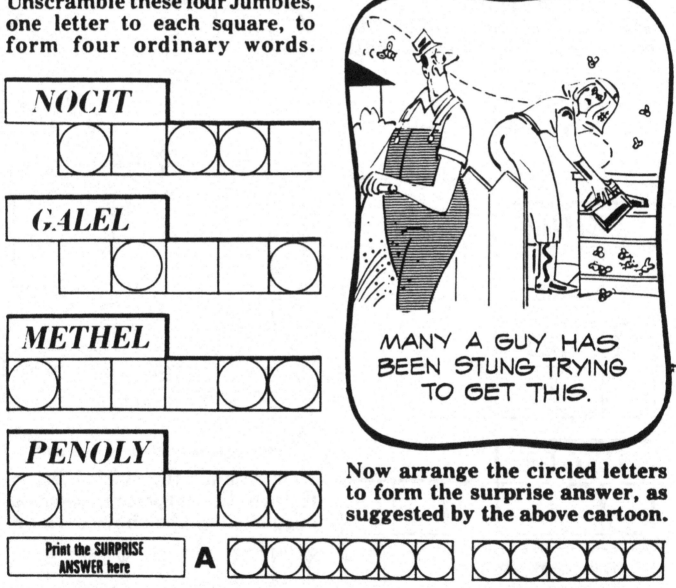

# JUMBLE®

Unscramble these four Jumbles, one letter to each square, to form four ordinary words.

**BORNI**

**TULFE**

**REPIME**

**SOLFIS**

Careful!

WHERE YOU HAVE MOUNTAIN RANGES YOU MIGHT ALSO FIND THIS.

Now arrange the circled letters to form the surprise answer, as suggested by the above cartoon.

Print the SURPRISE ANSWER here

# JUMBLE®

Unscramble these four Jumbles,
one letter to each square, to
form four ordinary words.

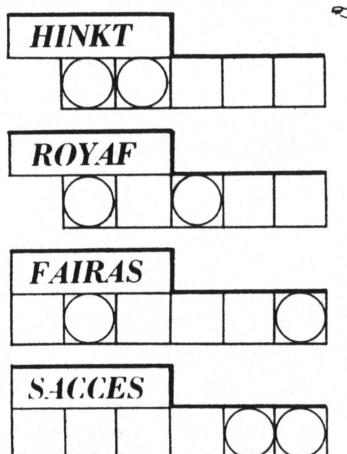

HINKT

ROYAF

FAIRAS

SACCES

Print the SURPRISE ANSWER here

A

THIS MIGHT BE
CONSPICUOUS IN SOME
UNDERWATER PLAY.

Now arrange the circled letters
to form the surprise answer, as
suggested by the above cartoon.

14

# JUMBLE®

Unscramble these four Jumbles,
one letter to each square, to
form four ordinary words.

GLUBY

CUIJE

TEAREA

ROGDEC

Print the SURPRISE ANSWER here

WHAT A BRIGHT
GOLD DIGGER'S
WEAPON MIGHT BE.

Now arrange the circled letters
to form the surprise answer, as
suggested by the above cartoon.

HER " ◯◯◯ - ◯◯◯ "

▲▼▲▼▲▼▲▼▲▼▲▼▲▼▲▼▲▼▲▼▲▼▲▼▲▼▲▼▲

# JUMBLE®

Unscramble these four Jumbles,
one letter to each square, to
form four ordinary words.

**RYPAH**

**KANTE**

**YERSIM**

**RYLAIF**

What do
you think?

WHAT THE GUY WHO
CLAIMED HE COULD
READ WOMEN LIKE A
BOOK MUST HAVE BEEN.

Now arrange the circled letters
to form the surprise answer, as
suggested by the above cartoon.

Print the SURPRISE ANSWER here

**A**

# JUMBLE®

Unscramble these four Jumbles, one letter to each square, to form four ordinary words.

**YAASS**

**HOTYM**

**TEAZOL**

**PINGYT**

WHAT A BABY MIGHT BE IN WARM WEATHER

Now arrange the circled letters to form the surprise answer, as suggested by the above cartoon.

Print the SURPRISE ANSWER here

A

▲▼▲▼▲▼▲▼▲▼▲▼▲▼▲▼▲▼▲▼▲▼▲▼▲▼

# JUMBLE®

Unscramble these four Jumbles,
one letter to each square, to
form four ordinary words.

**DYRYL**

**OINES**

**GATHIL**

**HINCLE**

Let's borrow from Grandpa

THESE KIDS MIGHT MAKE *THE RICH LEND.*

Now arrange the circled letters
to form the surprise answer, as
suggested by the above cartoon.

Print the SURPRISE ANSWER here **THE** ◯◯◯◯◯◯◯◯

18

# JUMBLE®

Unscramble these four Jumbles, one letter to each square, to form four ordinary words.

**RALVO**

**GEFUD**

**BROCAN**

**RIMMOE**

SPLASH!

WHEN IT'S WET, GET UNDER IT!

Now arrange the circled letters to form the surprise answer, as suggested by the above cartoon.

Print the SURPRISE ANSWER here

# JUMBLE®

Unscramble these four Jumbles, one letter to each square, to form four ordinary words.

**DANAP**

**YIKTT**

**DONBEY**

**RYSLIG**

WHAT THE PIG SAID AS THE SUN GREW HOTTER.

Now arrange the circled letters to form the surprise answer, as suggested by the above cartoon.

Print the SURPRISE ANSWER here

I'M ⬭⬭⬭⬭⬭⬭'

# JUMBLE®

Unscramble these four Jumbles,
one letter to each square, to
form four ordinary words.

**TEBER**

**POREA**

**MANIAE**

**CHOPON**

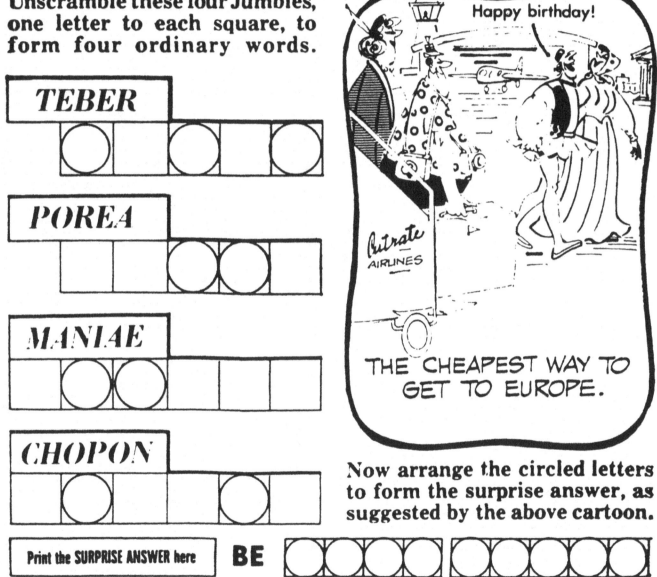

Happy birthday!

Cutrate
AIRLINES

THE CHEAPEST WAY TO
GET TO EUROPE.

Now arrange the circled letters
to form the surprise answer, as
suggested by the above cartoon.

Print the SURPRISE ANSWER here

**BE**

# JUMBLE®

Unscramble these four Jumbles,
one letter to each square, to
form four ordinary words.

**YETID**

**SABSY**

**LEHBED**

**PRUSHE**

Hard work; good soil; water . . .

Green thumb?

AT THE BOTTOM OF
SUCCESSFUL GARDENING.

Now arrange the circled letters
to form the surprise answer, as
suggested by the above cartoon.

Print the SURPRISE ANSWER here

# JUMBLE.

Unscramble these four Jumbles,
one letter to each square, to
form four ordinary words.

ASAIL

HORTT

KEBTUC

MEDOCY

Print the SURPRISE ANSWER here

WHAT A BOY WHO
HATES BOOKS MIGHT
PREFER TO DO.

Now arrange the circled letters
to form the surprise answer, as
suggested by the above cartoon.

23

# JUMBLE®

Unscramble these four Jumbles, one letter to each square, to form four ordinary words.

LIGUT

NEMOD

LABERV

CRAIPY

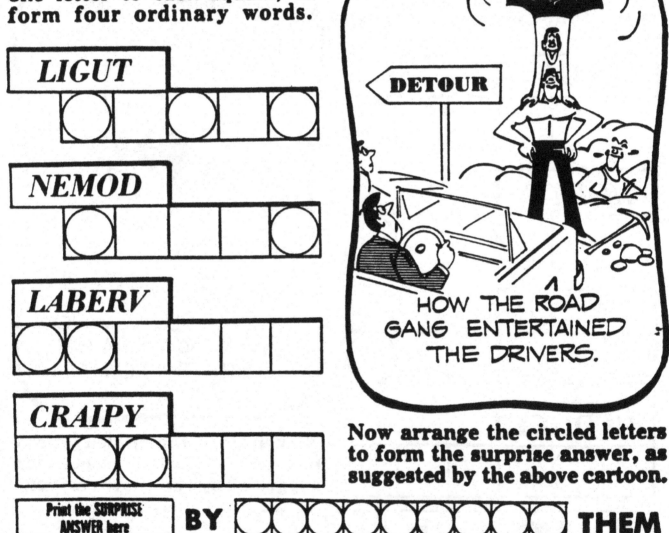

DETOUR

HOW THE ROAD GANG ENTERTAINED THE DRIVERS.

Now arrange the circled letters to form the surprise answer, as suggested by the above cartoon.

Print the SURPRISE ANSWER here

BY ⭕⭕⭕⭕⭕⭕⭕⭕⭕ THEM

# JUMBLE®

Unscramble these four Jumbles, one letter to each square, to form four ordinary words.

**LOOGI**

**RAVOL**

**TALMEL**

**GINCHA**

Print the SURPRISE ANSWER here

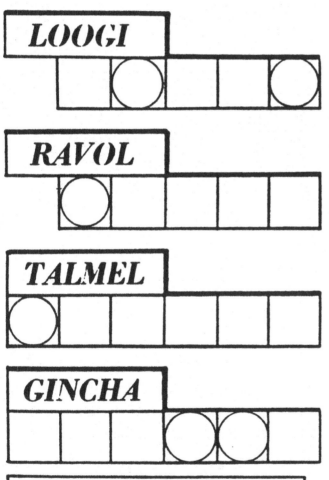

Can't wait to use our new swimming pool

WHY LEAVING YOUR OLD HOME MIGHT BE EMOTIONALLY DISTURBING.

Now arrange the circled letters to form the surprise answer, as suggested by the above cartoon.

IT'S " ⬡⬡⬡⬡⬡⬡ "

# JUMBLE®

Unscramble these four Jumbles,
one letter to each square, to
form four ordinary words.

**JABON**

**PEDYT**

**NAHLED**

**SNEFTA**

Tonight again?

THEY SOMETIMES WORK
AROUND THE CLOCK
ON THE FARM.

Now arrange the circled letters
to form the surprise answer, as
suggested by the above cartoon.

" "

Print the SURPRISE ANSWER here

# JUMBLE®

Unscramble these four Jumbles,
one letter to each square, to
form four ordinary words.

VENOL

PIGER

BROSAB

DAYNIT

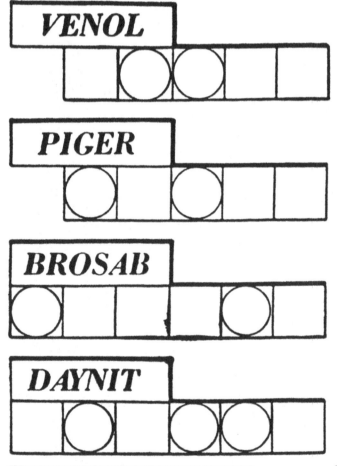

PROVIDES THE
MAIN COURSE ON
BOARD SHIP.

Now arrange the circled letters
to form the surprise answer, as
suggested by the above cartoon.

Print the SURPRISE ANSWER here

THE ◯◯◯◯◯◯◯◯◯◯

▲▽▲▽▲▽▲▽▲▽▲▽▲▽▲▽▲▽▲▽▲▽▲▽▲▽▲▽▲▽▲▽

# JUMBLE®

Unscramble these four Jumbles,
one letter to each square, to
form four ordinary words.

**ANUDT**

**PAMCH**

**SMIBUT**

**TINVER**

What beautiful
scenery!

BACKGROUND MATERIAL
FOR AN ARTIST.

Now arrange the circled letters
to form the surprise answer, as
suggested by the above cartoon.

Print the SURPRISE ANSWER here

# JUMBLE®

Unscramble these four Jumbles, one letter to each square, to form four ordinary words.

**NYOME**

**UNDOB**

**EMFONT**

**GANDIL**

Come out in the garden!

How beautiful!

Now arrange the circled letters to form the surprise answer, as suggested by the above cartoon.

Print the SURPRISE ANSWER here

# JUMBLE®

Unscramble these four Jumbles, one letter to each square, to form four ordinary words.

**PHACT**

**HIWSS**

**PIMAGE**

**GREJIG**

SEVERAL IN A FLIGHT.

Now arrange the circled letters to form the surprise answer, as suggested by the above cartoon.

Print the SURPRISE ANSWER here

# JUMBLE®

Unscramble these four Jumbles,
one letter to each square, to
form four ordinary words.

**DESTE**

**YAILG**

**BASHUM**

**CYMALL**

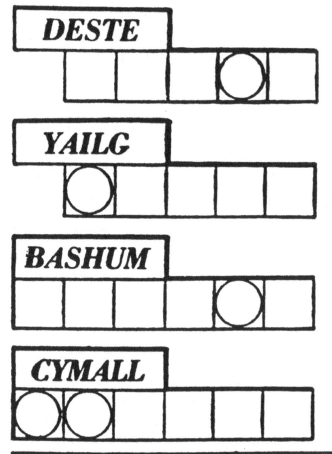

Cover up!

ZOO

NO SUN-BATHING

MIGHT BE BARRED
IN SOME PARKS.

Now arrange the circled letters
to form the surprise answer, as
suggested by the above cartoon.

Print the SURPRISE ANSWER here

31

▲▽▲▽▲▽▲▽▲▽▲▽▲▽▲▽▲▽▲▽▲▽▲▽▲▽▲▽▲▽▲▽

# JUMBLE®

Unscramble these four Jumbles,
one letter to each square, to
form four ordinary words.

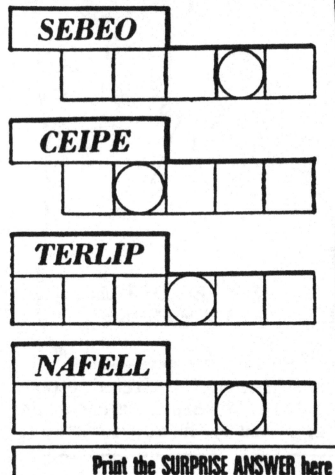

**SEBEO**

**CEIPE**

**TERLIP**

**NAFELL**

Print the SURPRISE ANSWER here

AN EDIBLE PART
OF POPPIES THAT
MANY BECOME
ADDICTED TO.

Now arrange the circled letters
to form the surprise answer, as
suggested by the above cartoon.

"◯◯◯◯"

# JUMBLE ®

Unscramble these four Jumbles,
one letter to each square, to
form four ordinary words.

**STRYT**

**ESING**

**LUBOSE**

**RETAUM**

Print the SURPRISE ANSWER here

Won't you
come to my
studio?

ONE WHO WON'T STAND
FOR BEING PAINTED.

Now arrange the circled letters
to form the surprise answer, as
suggested by the above cartoon.

A

# DAILY

## SUMMER FUN

### JUMBLE®

# JUMBLE®

Unscramble these four Jumbles, one letter to each square, to form four ordinary words.

**CASEE**

**ATAGE**

**UMSCAP**

**DILVER**

COULD BE THE PRICE OF HIRING A PRIVATE GUIDE TO TAKE YOU MOUNTAIN CLIMBING.

Now arrange the circled letters to form the surprise answer, as suggested by the above cartoon.

**Print answer here:**

# JUMBLE®

Unscramble these four Jumbles,
one letter to each square, to form
four ordinary words.

AZERC

MAGDO

NAANAB

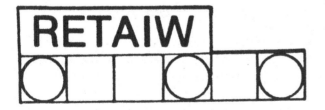

RETAIW

WHAT THE DESERT
RAT SAID TO
HIS PAL.

Now arrange the circled letters to
form the surprise answer, as suggested by the above cartoon.

Answer: ⬡⬡⬡⬡⬡ WE ⬡⬡⬡⬡⬡⬡ DO?

# JUMBLE.

Unscramble these four Jumbles, one letter to each square, to form four ordinary words.

**GOGER**

**MUSIN**

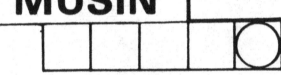
**LEUXED**

**TIMCAP**

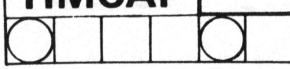

HOW WITCH DOCTORS KEEP FIT.

Now arrange the circled letters to form the surprise answer, as suggested by the above cartoon.

*Answer here:* **THEY** "  "

38

# JUMBLE®

Unscramble these four Jumbles, one letter to each square, to form four ordinary words.

DEPIT

HAFFC

VAHBEE

TEGOTH

WHAT THE PROUD GIRAFFE KEPT.

Now arrange the circled letters to form the surprise answer, as suggested by the above cartoon.

**Print answer here:** HER ⬡⬡⬡⬡ ⬡⬡⬡⬡

# JUMBLE®

Unscramble these four Jumbles, one letter to each square, to form four ordinary words.

WONGI

YERME

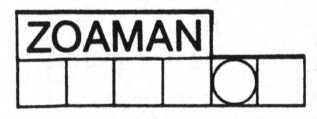

ZOAMAN

DROBIF

Don't look!

WHAT YOU MIGHT FIND IN BORNEO— ON A NATIVE.

Now arrange the circled letters to form the surprise answer, as suggested by the above cartoon.

Print answer here:

# JUMBLE®

Unscramble these four Jumbles,
one letter to each square, to form
four ordinary words.

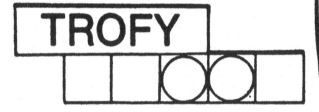

TROFY

DUTEE

NORGAD

VORGEN

WHAT HE SAID
WHEN ASKED
WHETHER HE HAD
LIKED COLLEGE,

Now arrange the circled letters to
form the surprise answer, as suggested by the above cartoon.

Print answer here:  A ""

41

▲▽▲▽▲▽▲▽▲▽▲▽▲▽▲▽▲▽▲▽▲▽▲▽▲▽▲▽▲

# JUMBLE®

Unscramble these four Jumbles,
one letter to each square, to form
four ordinary words.

CLUHG

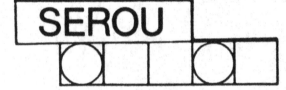

SEROU

PATELA

BEGBIT

WHAT BATHING
GIRLS MIGHT BE.

Now arrange the circled letters to
form the surprise answer, as suggested by the above cartoon.

Answer: " IN ⬡⬡⬡⬡⬡⬡ ⬡⬡⬡⬡ "

▲▽▲▽▲▽▲▽▲▽▲▽▲▽▲▽▲▽▲▽▲▽▲▽▲▽▲▽▲▽

# JUMBLE.

Unscramble these four Jumbles,
one letter to each square, to form
four ordinary words.

WHAT "TEQUILA" IS.

**MIDUH**

**ELVOG**

**ICETOX**

**GOPINE**

Now arrange the circled letters to
form the surprise answer, as suggested by the above cartoon.

Answer: THE "⬭⬭⬭⬭⬭" OF ⬭⬭⬭⬭⬭⬭⬭

# JUMBLE®

Unscramble these four Jumbles,
one letter to each square, to form
four ordinary words.

WYSON

TELOX

CEPPIT

LAMDAY

ONE PAW OF A BIG
LION COULD BE A
DANGEROUS ONE.

Now arrange the circled letters to
form the surprise answer, as suggested by the above cartoon.

Print answer here: " ⬚⬚⬚⬚⬚⬚⬚ "

44

# JUMBLE.

Unscramble these four Jumbles,
one letter to each square, to form
four ordinary words.

**SHECS**

**TRAFC**

**BROIMD**

**ENVARG**

THREATENED TO
RAIN ON THE ACTORS
AT THE OUTDOOR
THEATER.

Now arrange the circled letters to
form the surprise answer, as suggested by the above cartoon.

*Print answer here:* "  "

45

# JUMBLE®

Unscramble these four Jumbles, one letter to each square, to form four ordinary words.

**LUTEX**

**BOVAR**

**DIASUN**

**TEESHE**

YOU AND I AND NO ONE ELSE!

Now arrange the circled letters to form the surprise answer, as suggested by the above cartoon.

Print answer here:

# JUMBLE.

Unscramble these four Jumbles, one letter to each square, to form four ordinary words.

**HUBSY**

**DYRYL**

**TASHAG**

**BEFLAD**
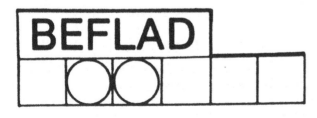

WHAT YOU WOULD EXPECT TO FIND PLENTY OF IN A MILITARY BAND COMPOSED MAINLY OF OFFICERS.

Now arrange the circled letters to form the surprise answer, as suggested by the above cartoon.

*Print answer here:* "  "

# JUMBLE.

Unscramble these four Jumbles, one letter to each square, to form four ordinary words.

**KIMPS**

**BYRIN**

**EXVONC**

**NUCHAH**

Aren't you supposed to be cleaning out the garage?

WHAT TIME AND GRIME DO.

Now arrange the circled letters to form the surprise answer, as suggested by the above cartoon.

**Print answer here:**

# JUMBLE®

Unscramble these four Jumbles,
one letter to each square, to form
four ordinary words.

**KADEB**

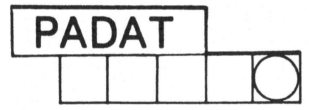
**PADAT**

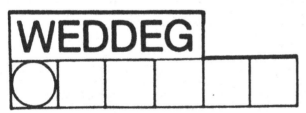
**WEDDEG**

**HASRIG**

WHAT "CHANGED" WHEN
THE SNOW MELTED?

Now arrange the circled letters to
form the surprise answer, as suggested by the above cartoon.

*Print answer here:*

49

# JUMBLE®

Unscramble these four Jumbles,
one letter to each square, to form
four ordinary words.

GEREM

ROHNO

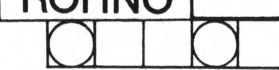

WELDIM

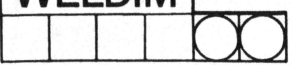

BOSULE

They look healthy in
body and mind

WHAT WORD IS IT
FROM WHICH THE
WHOLE MAY BE
TAKEN, AND YET
SOME WILL BE LEFT?

Now arrange the circled letters to
form the surprise answer, as suggested by the above cartoon.

Answer here: "◯◯◯◯◯◯◯◯◯"

# JUMBLE.

Unscramble these four Jumbles,
one letter to each square, to form
four ordinary words.

## RYKUM

## LEEBI

## ENLOOD

## DORINO

Tall and
willowy

THE EGOTIST'S
FAVORITE FIGURE.

Now arrange the circled letters to
form the surprise answer, as suggested by the above cartoon.

*Print answer here:*

# JUMBLE.

Unscramble these four Jumbles, one letter to each square, to form four ordinary words.

ROCKA

KEDAB

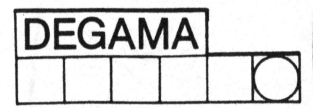

DEGAMA

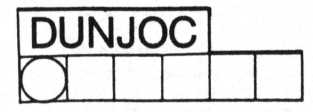

DUNJOC

CRACKED WHEN IT'S HEARD.

Now arrange the circled letters to form the surprise answer, as suggested by the above cartoon.

Print answer here:

52

# JUMBLE®

Unscramble these four Jumbles,
one letter to each square, to form
four ordinary words.

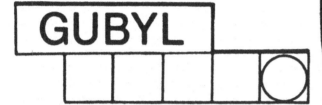

GUBYL

SYRTT

LOUBED

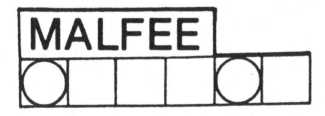

MALFEE

HOW TO RELAX
COMPLETELY.

Now arrange the circled letters to
form the surprise answer, as suggested by the above cartoon.

Answer here: "☐☐☐☐ – ☐☐☐☐☐"

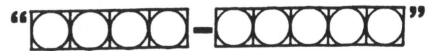

# JUMBLE ®

Unscramble these four Jumbles, one letter to each square, to form four ordinary words.

**LYSHY**

**TUSEG**

**LEABED**

**HORKES**

THEY SHOULD IMPROVE THE VIEW.

Now arrange the circled letters to form the surprise answer, as suggested by the above cartoon.

*Print answer here:*

# JUMBLE.

Unscramble these four Jumbles,
one letter to each square, to form
four ordinary words.

YENEM

ZARUE

TONBEN

BOLTAC

LEATHER GOODS    FOOD

SOUNDS LIKE
A GOOD
HIDING PLACE.

Now arrange the circled letters to
form the surprise answer, as suggested by the above cartoon.

Print answer here: A

55

# JUMBLE.

Unscramble these four Jumbles,
one letter to each square, to form
four ordinary words.

PLOIT

OMBUG

VAINED

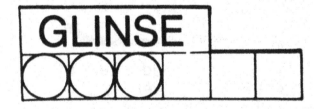

GLINSE

SOUNDED LIKE SOME
OLD-FASHIONED
NECKING THAT
MIGHT HAVE CAUSED
A "STIR."

Now arrange the circled letters to
form the surprise answer, as suggested by the above cartoon.

Print answer here: "  "

56

# JUMBLE.

Unscramble these four Jumbles,
one letter to each square, to form
four ordinary words.

**NAHEN**

**PAUNC**

**BELUCK**

**SLICHE**

WHAT THE
BATHING
BEAUTY WAS.

Now arrange the circled letters to
form the surprise answer, as suggested by the above cartoon.

*Answer here:* A

# JUMBLE®

Unscramble these four Jumbles,
one letter to each square, to form
four ordinary words.

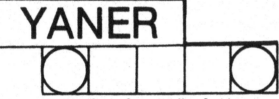

**YANER**

**SNAIB**

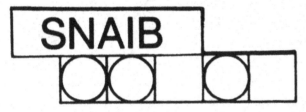

**LEARNY**

**SUDJAT**

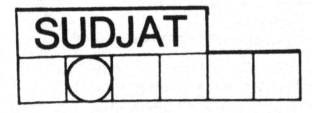

IF TODAY'S JUMBLE
SEEMS DIFFICULT,
SAVE IT FOR THIS.

Now arrange the circled letters to
form the surprise answer, as suggested by the above cartoon.

Answer: A " ◯◯◯◯◯◯ " ◯◯◯

# JUMBLE®

Unscramble these four Jumbles,
one letter to each square, to form
four ordinary words.

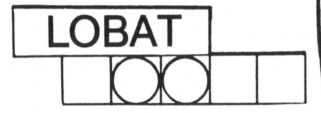

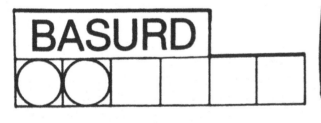

GOES UP AFTER
A PERIOD OF
INFLATION.

Now arrange the circled letters to
form the surprise answer, as suggested by the above cartoon.

Print answer here: A

59

▲▽▲▽▲▽▲▽▲▽▲▽▲▽▲▽▲▽▲▽▲▽▲▽▲▽▲▽

# JUMBLE®

Unscramble these four Jumbles,
one letter to each square, to form
four ordinary words.

**UNERP**

**VIRTE**

**SEMIED**

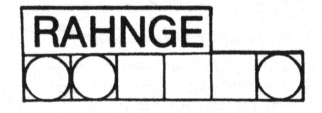

**RAHNGE**

REALLY GOES
AGAINST THE
FARMER'S GRAIN.

Now arrange the circled letters to
form the surprise answer, as suggested by the above cartoon.

Print answer here:

60

# JUMBLE.

Unscramble these four Jumbles,
one letter to each square, to form
four ordinary words.

KEROP

VURCE

SYTHAN

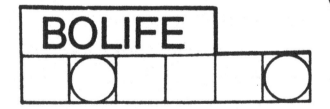

BOLIFE

I wonder
who took
them. . .

LITTLE BO-PEEP
LOST HER SHEEP
BECAUSE SHE
HAD THIS.

Now arrange the circled letters to
form the surprise answer, as suggested by the above cartoon.

Answer: A "◯◯◯◯◯◯" WITH ◯◯◯

▲▼▲▼▲▼▲▼▲▼▲▼▲▼▲▼▲▼▲▼▲▼▲▼▲▼▲▼▲▼

# JUMBLE®

Unscramble these four Jumbles,
one letter to each square, to form
four ordinary words.

MYDUP

BIRAB

TEAREA

IT'S GOOD-BY
TO A GIRL IN
PARIS.

DRUGED

Now arrange the circled letters to
form the surprise answer, as suggested by the above cartoon.

*Print answer here:* "⬡⬡⬡⬡⬡"

# JUMBLE®

Unscramble these four Jumbles, one letter to each square, to form four ordinary words.

**GEBOF**

**SYSOM**

**HARTOU**

**DENORM**

THEY PROVIDE A MEANS OF SUPPORT FOR THOSE WHO RAISE FLOWERS.

Now arrange the circled letters to form the surprise answer, as suggested by the above cartoon.

*Print answer here:*

63

▲▼▲▼▲▼▲▼▲▼▲▼▲▼▲▼▲▼▲▼▲▼▲▼▲▼▲▼▲▼▲▼

# JUMBLE.

Unscramble these four Jumbles,
one letter to each square, to form
four ordinary words.

**YUSUR**

**CHITH**

**COHBOR**

**LIRIXE**

Beat it!

WHAT THE PAINTER
GAVE HIM.

Now arrange the circled letters to
form the surprise answer, as suggested by the above cartoon.

Print answer here: ☐☐☐ " ☐☐☐☐☐ "

# JUMBLE.

Unscramble these four Jumbles,
one letter to each square, to form
four ordinary words.

EBBIR

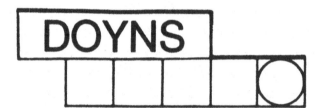
DOYNS

SAMOUF

REPERF

WHAT HE SAID
WHEN INFLATION
THREATENED TO
WIPE OUT HIS
NEST EGG.

Now arrange the circled letters to
form the surprise answer, as suggested by the above cartoon.

 *Answer here:* IT'S  THE _____!

# JUMBLE.

Unscramble these four Jumbles,
one letter to each square, to form
four ordinary words.

GOLIO

LOUFT

TIMLEG

FLAHBE

WHAT A BABY
BIRD EXPECTS
MAMA TO DO AT
DINNERTIME.

Now arrange the circled letters to
form the surprise answer, as suggested by the above cartoon.

Answer here:  THE

66

# JUMBLE®

Unscramble these four Jumbles,
one letter to each square, to form
four ordinary words.

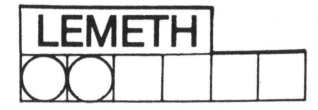

BOARR

DYSUK

CADAFE

LEMETH

HOW THE MILKING
CONTEST
ENDED UP.

Now arrange the circled letters to
form the surprise answer, as suggested by the above cartoon.

Answer: IN "  "

# JUMBLE.

Unscramble these four Jumbles,
one letter to each square, to form
four ordinary words.

**MICER**

**LUMGO**

**MOURUQ**

**SNIBAH**

IN WHICH IT'S
DIFFICULT TO ROW—
WHEN YOU "MANIPULATE"
HUGE OARS.

Now arrange the circled letters to
form the surprise answer, as suggested by the above cartoon.

Answer here: A "◯◯◯◯◯ ◯◯◯"

# JUMBLE®

Unscramble these four Jumbles,
one letter to each square, to form
four ordinary words.

MYNEE

DAMMA

TUILGY

DESEEC

THE BEST
LINE TO HOOK
A WOMAN WITH.

Now arrange the circled letters to
form the surprise answer, as suggested by the above cartoon.

Answer here: "◯◯◯◯◯◯ – ◯◯◯◯"

# JUMBLE.

Unscramble these four Jumbles,
one letter to each square, to form
four ordinary words.

TRUPE

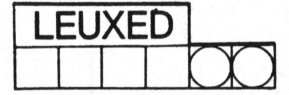

ROFOL

LEUXED

GREESY

AT THE SEASHORE,
YOUR COMPOSURE
IS OFTEN DISTRACTED
BY THIS.

Now arrange the circled letters to
form the surprise answer, as suggested by the above cartoon.

Print answer here:

# JUMBLE.

Unscramble these four Jumbles,
one letter to each square, to form
four ordinary words.

ORFEC

HIDUM

WARTOD

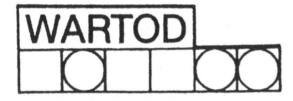

WHEPEN

Not fit for
man nor beast

WHAT A SUDDEN
CLOUDBURST IS.

Now arrange the circled letters to
form the surprise answer, as suggested by the above cartoon.

Answer here: A " ◯◯◯◯◯ " ◯◯◯◯

# JUMBLE®

Unscramble these four Jumbles,
one letter to each square, to form
four ordinary words.

CENEP

TOCET

NAHZIG

HUCCOR

FISHING MAY BE
A "DISEASE," BUT
IT'S NOT NECES-
SARILY THIS.

Now arrange the circled letters to
form the surprise answer, as suggested by the above cartoon.

Print answer here: "  "

# JUMBLE.

Unscramble these four Jumbles, one letter to each square, to form four ordinary words.

EAPEY

RAWFE

BETHIL

VARQUE

WHY SHE DIVED INTO THE SEA.

Now arrange the circled letters to form the surprise answer, as suggested by the above cartoon.

Answer: TO GET A [ ⃝⃝⃝⃝ ] IN HER [ ⃝⃝⃝⃝ ]

▲▽▲▽▲▽▲▽▲▽▲▽▲▽▲▽▲▽▲▽▲▽▲▽▲▽▲▽▲▽

# JUMBLE®

Unscramble these four Jumbles,
one letter to each square, to form
four ordinary words.

**LIEBE**

**YURLT**

**KEWRAH**

**EVITLY**

SOME PEOPLE WHO THINK THEY'RE "IN THE SWIM" ARE JUST THIS.

Now arrange the circled letters to
form the surprise answer, as suggested by the above cartoon.

Print answer here:

74

# JUMBLE®

Unscramble these four Jumbles,
one letter to each square, to form
four ordinary words.

**NOOZE**

**MAALL**

**DIPTUN**

**YAQUES**

LOVES SKIN
DIVING.

Now arrange the circled letters to
form the surprise answer, as suggested by the above cartoon.

Print answer here: A

# JUMBLE.

Unscramble these four Jumbles,
one letter to each square, to form
four ordinary words.

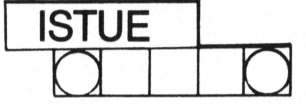
ISTUE

TASHY

PRUMAK

MASTIG

WHAT A HULA
DANCE IS.

Now arrange the circled letters to
form the surprise answer, as suggested by the above cartoon.

Answer: A ⬚⬚⬚⬚⬚ IN THE ⬚⬚⬚⬚⬚

# JUMBLE®

Unscramble these four Jumbles,
one letter to each square, to form
four ordinary words.

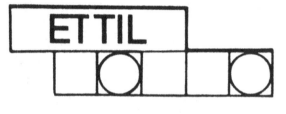

ETTIL

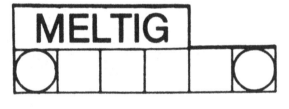

GORRI

MELTIG

NIWWON

WHAT HAPPENED
TO THE BELL THAT
FELL INTO THE
WATER?

Now arrange the circled letters to
form the surprise answer, as suggested by the above cartoon.

Answer: IT WAS " ⬡⬡⬡⬡⬡⬡⬡ " ⬡⬡⬡

# JUMBLE®

Unscramble these four Jumbles,
one letter to each square, to form
four ordinary words.

PROAN

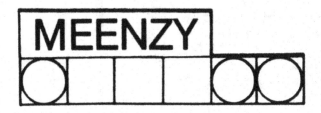

DAHYN

MEENZY

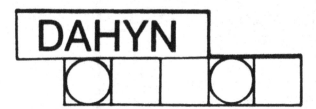

ZARABA

WHAT THE
PICNICKERS WERE.

Now arrange the circled letters to
form the surprise answer, as suggested by the above cartoon.

Print answer here: "  "

# JUMBLE.®

Unscramble these four Jumbles,
one letter to each square, to form
four ordinary words.

YILCI

KARCC

DAMMAN

TARGEY

WHEN THEY TOOK THAT
TROPICAL VACATION,
THEY APPARENTLY
WERE SAVING THEIR
MONEY FOR THIS.

Now arrange the circled letters to
form the surprise answer, as suggested by the above cartoon.

Print answer here: A

▲▼▲▼▲▼▲▼▲▼▲▼▲▼▲▼▲▼▲▼▲▼▲▼▲▼▲

# JUMBLE®

Unscramble these four Jumbles,
one letter to each square, to form
four ordinary words.

SOINY

MENGO

YABSUW

TEKLET

EVEN MORE FUN
THAN HAVING A
VACATION IS
HAVING THIS.

Now arrange the circled letters to
form the surprise answer, as suggested by the above cartoon.

Answer: THE ⬡⬡⬡⬡ ⬡⬡⬡⬡ ⬡⬡⬡

# JUMBLE®

Unscramble these four Jumbles,
one letter to each square, to form
four ordinary words.

TOBEG

GYDUP

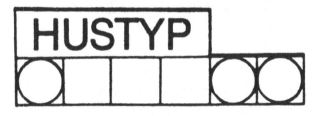
HUSTYP

NUCCOR

WHAT THE POOPED
KANGAROO WAS.

Now arrange the circled letters to
form the surprise answer, as suggested by the above cartoon.

Answer: "  " OF "  "

# JUMBLE.

Unscramble these four Jumbles,
one letter to each square, to form
four ordinary words.

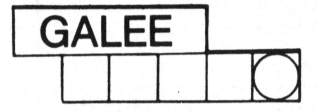

GALEE

SYSAG

TINEKT

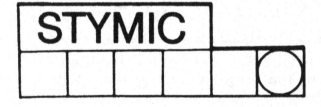

STYMIC

WHAT THAT LONG
TOUR MADE HIM.

Now arrange the circled letters to
form the surprise answer, as suggested by the above cartoon.

Print answer here: " ⬡⬡⬡ " ⬡⬡⬡⬡⬡

# JUMBLE.

Unscramble these four Jumbles,
one letter to each square, to form
four ordinary words.

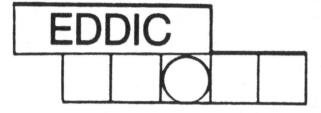

EDDIC

DYPET

TEAQUE

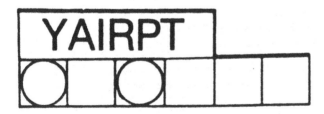

YAIRPT

WHAT'S THE
PROBLEM WITH
SHORT SKIRTS?

Now arrange the circled letters to
form the surprise answer, as suggested by the above cartoon.

Print answer here: THE " _____ "

▲▼▲▼▲▼▲▼▲▼▲▼▲▼▲▼▲▼▲▼▲▼▲▼▲▼▲▼▲▼

# JUMBLE.

Unscramble these four Jumbles,
one letter to each square, to form
four ordinary words.

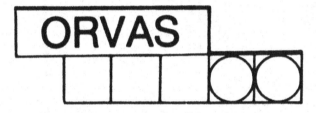

**ORVAS**

**TWAHR**

**WOFELL**

**TEXMEP**

WHAT HIS NEIGHBOR
SAID WHEN HE
SHOWED OFF HIS NEW
LAWN EQUIPMENT.

Now arrange the circled letters to
form the surprise answer, as suggested by the above cartoon.

Answer: " ◯◯◯◯◯ " ◯◯◯◯◯ TO YOU

84

# JUMBLE®

Unscramble these four Jumbles, one letter to each square, to form four ordinary words.

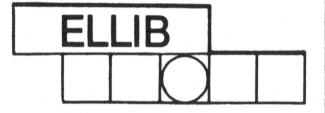

ELLIB

ALCAN

DELBOH

WEDDAN

WHAT THE RABBITS WHO WERE PLAYING IN THE ONION PATCH HAD.

Now arrange the circled letters to form the surprise answer, as suggested by the above cartoon.

*Print answer here:*  "  "

▲▼▲▼▲▼▲▼▲▼▲▼▲▼▲▼▲▼▲▼▲▼▲▼▲▼▲▼▲

# JUMBLE®

Unscramble these four Jumbles, one letter to each square, to form four ordinary words.

OCCIL

TOAQU

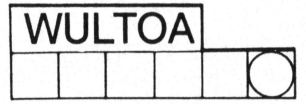

WULTOA

RYLURF

THE GONDOLIER MAY BE SERENADING YOU, BUT HE'S READY FOR THIS.

Now arrange the circled letters to form the surprise answer, as suggested by the above cartoon.

*Print answer here:*  "  "

# JUMBLE®

Unscramble these four Jumbles, one letter to each square, to form four ordinary words.

GOOLI

CASHO

CARGIL

BRANER

Soon we'll run out of room for them

WHAT KIND OF A PLACE WAS THAT RABBIT FARM?

Now arrange the circled letters to form the surprise answer, as suggested by the above cartoon.

Answer: "⬡⬡⬡⬡⬡ – ⬡⬡⬡⬡⬡⬡⬡⬡"

Unscramble these four Jumbles,
one letter to each square, to form
four ordinary words.

HIGEW

ROWEB

DEHEAB

LARCOR

WHAT ONE BIRD
SAID TO THE OTHER.

Now arrange the circled letters to
form the surprise answer, as suggested by the above cartoon.

Answer: " ⬚⬚⬚⬚⬚ WE ⬚⬚⬚⬚⬚ ?"

88

# JUMBLE®

Unscramble these four Jumbles,
one letter to each square, to form
four ordinary words.

USIGE

INJOG

LEMDEY

NULKIE

THERE WAS PLENTY
OF THIS WHEN A
QUARREL BROKE OUT
IN THE PIGPEN.

Now arrange the circled letters to
form the surprise answer, as suggested by the above cartoon.

Answer:

89

# JUMBLE.

Unscramble these four Jumbles,
one letter to each square, to form
four ordinary words.

FRASC

WELJE

DRAWZI

KEBTUC

IF A HUNGRY
SHARK IS IN THE
NEIGHBORHOOD,
FEED HIM THIS.

Now arrange the circled letters to
form the surprise answer, as suggested by the above cartoon.

Answer:

# JUMBLE®

Unscramble these four Jumbles,
one letter to each square, to form
four ordinary words.

CARTT

LALAM

NECCIS

SYTTUR

WHAT THOSE OLD SAILING -VESSELS MUST HAVE PROVIDED.

Now arrange the circled letters to
form the surprise answer, as suggested by the above cartoon.

Answer:

91

# JUMBLE®

Unscramble these four Jumbles,
one letter to each square, to form
four ordinary words.

ENAKO

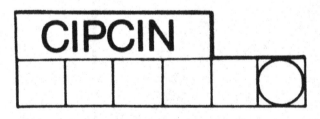

TAABE

CIPCIN

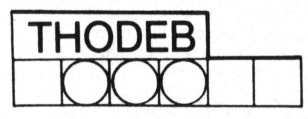

THODEB

WHERE THAT STERN
CAPTAIN ALWAYS
STOOD, NATURALLY.

Now arrange the circled letters to
form the surprise answer, as suggested by the above cartoon.

Answer: AT THE ⬡⬡⬡⬡ OF THE ⬡⬡⬡⬡

# JUMBLE®

Unscramble these four Jumbles,
one letter to each square, to form
four ordinary words.

NOTIX

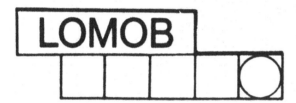

LOMOB

REEVER

HANCUL

IT'S SOMETIMES
A CRIME TO CATCH
FISH HERE, BUT
MORE OFTEN THIS.

Now arrange the circled letters to
form the surprise answer, as suggested by the above cartoon.

Print answer here: A

▲▽▲▽▲▽▲▽▲▽▲▽▲▽▲▽▲▽▲▽▲▽▲▽▲▽▲▽

# JUMBLE®

Unscramble these four Jumbles,
one letter to each square, to form
four ordinary words.

SNACKS MEANT
TO REFRESH
OFTEN END
UP DOING THIS.

Now arrange the circled letters to
form the surprise answer, as suggested by the above cartoon.

Print answer here: "  "

# JUMBLE®

Unscramble these four Jumbles,
one letter to each square, to form
four ordinary words.

NAVER

OCHAM

TEFNIC

SOPPEO

CAN YOU TELL ME
WHAT NAPOLEON'S
ORIGIN WAS?

Now arrange the circled letters to
form the surprise answer, as suggested by the above cartoon.

Answer: "⬡⬡⬡⬡⬡⬡ - ⬡ - ⬡⬡⬡"

# JUMBLE®

Unscramble these four Jumbles, one letter to each square, to form four ordinary words.

**YUMMG**

**LYRUS**

**HATHEL**

**ENVORG**

You shoulda seen it

THE "ONE THAT GOT AWAY" WOULD HAVE BEEN BIGGER IF THE FISHERMAN HAD THIS.

Now arrange the circled letters to form the surprise answer, as suggested by the above cartoon.

Answer here:

# JUMBLE®

Unscramble these four Jumbles, one letter to each square, to form four ordinary words.

**TINAF**

**CIDDE**

**MIRNIF**

**STEJER**

Hey, fellows—can you help me out?

STOCKS

$

WHAT A SPONGER NEEDS IN ORDER TO KEEP AFLOAT.

Now arrange the circled letters to form the surprise answer, as suggested by the above cartoon.

Answer: A ⬡⬡⬡⬡ OF ⬡⬡⬡⬡⬡⬡⬡

# JUMBLE.

Unscramble these four Jumbles,
one letter to each square, to form
four ordinary words.

**DEEKY**

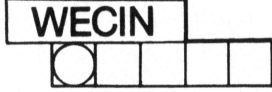

**WECIN**

**TINIVE**

**PEBSIC**

WHAT KIND OF A
GAME IS CROQUET?

Now arrange the circled letters to
form the surprise answer, as suggested by the above cartoon.

*Print answer here:* A "◯◯◯◯◯◯" ONE

# JUMBLE®

Unscramble these four Jumbles, one letter to each square, to form four ordinary words.

**HASQU**

**BARRO**

**YAGTIE**

**CLETOH**

I told you not to annoy the animals!

WHAT THE ZOOKEEPER SAID HIS LIFE WAS.

Now arrange the circled letters to form the surprise answer, as suggested by the above cartoon.

Print answer here:

▲▽▲▽▲▽▲▽▲▽▲▽▲▽▲▽▲▽▲▽▲▽▲▽▲▽▲▽▲▽▲

# JUMBLE®

Unscramble these four Jumbles, one letter to each square, to form four ordinary words.

KAHIK

RYPAH

SAQUEY

LUMUTT

WHAT A BELLY LAUGH IS.

Now arrange the circled letters to form the surprise answer, as suggested by the above cartoon.

Answer: A "⬡⬡⬡⬡⬡" ⬡⬡⬡⬡⬡

# JUMBLE.

Unscramble these four Jumbles, one letter to each square, to form four ordinary words.

DANAP

RIMON

YENKOD

CREEFI

WHERE CAN YOU BUY CAMEL'S MILK?

Tee hee

Now arrange the circled letters to form the surprise answer, as suggested by the above cartoon.

Answer: AT "⬡⬡⬡⬡⬡ – ⬡⬡⬡⬡⬡"
A

101

▲▼▲▼▲▼▲▼▲▼▲▼▲▼▲▼▲▼▲▼▲▼▲▼▲▼▲▼▲

# JUMBLE®

Unscramble these four Jumbles,
one letter to each square, to form
four ordinary words.

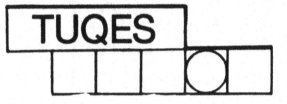

TUQES

GYKAW

TOENED

RELUSY

WHAT TO WEAR
WHEN WORKING
OUTDOORS.

Now arrange the circled letters to
form the surprise answer, as suggested by the above cartoon.

Answer: A " ◯◯◯◯ ◯◯◯◯◯ "

# JUMBLE.

Unscramble these four Jumbles, one letter to each square, to form four ordinary words.

**NOPUD**

**HOBUG**

**VERDIF**

**KRALTE**

WHAT CAUSED THE PUNCTURE IN THE TIRE?

Now arrange the circled letters to form the surprise answer, as suggested by the above cartoon.

Answer here: A ⬡⬡⬡⬡⬡ IN THE ⬡⬡⬡⬡

▲▽▲▽▲▽▲▽▲▽▲▽▲▽▲▽▲▽▲▽▲▽▲▽▲▽▲▽▲▽▲

# JUMBLE®

Unscramble these four Jumbles, one letter to each square, to form four ordinary words.

PODEK

NOOHR

GLUTLE

SHMAIF

WHAT A VISITOR TO HAWAII IS INTERESTED IN FINDING OUT ABOUT FIRST.

Now arrange the circled letters to form the surprise answer, as suggested by the above cartoon.

Answer: THE "◯◯◯" OF THE ◯◯◯◯

# JUMBLE.

Unscramble these four Jumbles,
one letter to each square, to form
four ordinary words.

**HEWIG**

**GLARN**

**DINTAB**

**LICKEF**

Sunny all day

WHETHER IT RAINED
OR NOT THE WEATHER
CASTER WAS THIS
MOST OF THE TIME.

Now arrange the circled letters to
form the surprise answer, as suggested by the above cartoon.

Print answer here:

▲▽▲▽▲▽▲▽▲▽▲▽▲▽▲▽▲▽▲▽▲▽▲▽▲▽▲▽▲

# JUMBLE.

Unscramble these four Jumbles,
one letter to each square, to form
four ordinary words.

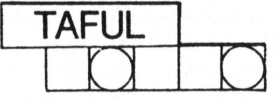

TAFUL

ROBIL

LYBBAF

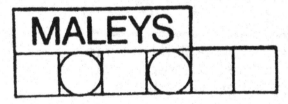

MALEYS

WHEN IS A BOAT
THE CHEAPEST?

Now arrange the circled letters to
form the surprise answer, as suggested by the above cartoon.

Answer: WHEN " ⭘⭘⭘⭘ " ⭘⭘⭘⭘
IT'S A

# JUMBLE.

Unscramble these four Jumbles, one letter to each square, to form four ordinary words.

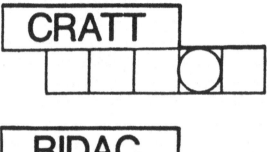

CRATT

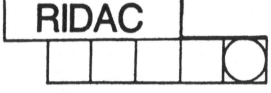

RIDAC

VOCENX

BELBUB

Got to get rid of this ham

WHAT THE INDIA RUBBER MAN AT THE CIRCUS GOT.

Now arrange the circled letters to form the surprise answer, as suggested by the above cartoon.

Print answer here:

▲▼▲▼▲▼▲▼▲▼▲▼▲▼▲▼▲▼▲▼▲▼▲▼▲

# JUMBLE®

Unscramble these four Jumbles,
one letter to each square, to form
four ordinary words.

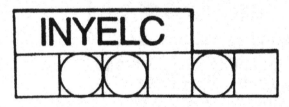

NOYGA

TANEC

KLUBEC

INYELC

WHAT HER
COMPANIONS
CALLED THAT
STUPID HEN.

Now arrange the circled letters to
form the surprise answer, as suggested by the above cartoon.

Print answer here: A

# JUMBLE.

Unscramble these four Jumbles, one letter to each square, to form four ordinary words.

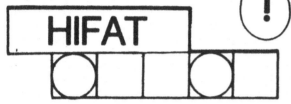

HIFAT

ORPYX

BALLOG

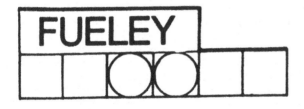

FUELEY

Two minutes early

WHY THE COP TURNED MUSICIAN GOT FIRED FROM THE BAND.

Now arrange the circled letters to form the surprise answer, as suggested by the above cartoon.

*Answer here:* HE WAS "   "

▲▼▲▼▲▼▲▼▲▼▲▼▲▼▲▼▲▼▲▼▲▼▲▼▲▼▲▼▲

# JUMBLE®

Unscramble these four Jumbles,
one letter to each square, to form
four ordinary words.

YOGGS

ENTAK

CUSSEN

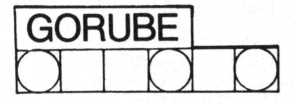

GORUBE

WHAT YOU'D EXPECT
TO HAVE FOR
BREAKFAST AT A
LIGHTHOUSE.

Now arrange the circled letters to
form the surprise answer, as suggested by the above cartoon.

Answer: "⬡⬡⬡⬡⬡⬡" & ⬡⬡⬡⬡

# JUMBLE®

Unscramble these four Jumbles,
one letter to each square, to form
four ordinary words.

NELLK

TOOBA

ZELPUZ

BREEMM

It's sure riding easy

WHAT SAILING
A BOAT ON A
NICE WINDY DAY
CAN BE.

Now arrange the circled letters to
form the surprise answer, as suggested by the above cartoon.

Print answer here:

▲▼▲▼▲▼▲▼▲▼▲▼▲▼▲▼▲▼▲▼▲▼▲▼▲▼▲▼▲▼

# JUMBLE.

Unscramble these four Jumbles, one letter to each square, to form four ordinary words.

**LIFUD**

**SLURY**

**JURNIY**

**HEABED**

What a dirty job!

But they interfere with navigation

A STERN NECESSITY ON A BOAT.

Now arrange the circled letters to form the surprise answer, as suggested by the above cartoon.

Print answer here: A ◯◯◯◯◯◯◯

112

# JUMBLE®

Unscramble these four Jumbles, one letter to each square, to form four ordinary words.

**ENUQE**

**LEELB**

**SIBOPH**

**PIMAGE**

A FISHERMAN SOME-TIMES STANDS STILL WHILE FISHING, BUT MORE OFTEN DOES THIS.

Now arrange the circled letters to form the surprise answer, as suggested by the above cartoon.

Print answer here:

▲▽▲▽▲▽▲▽▲▽▲▽▲▽▲▽▲▽▲▽▲▽▲▽▲▽▲▽

# JUMBLE.

Unscramble these four Jumbles, one letter to each square, to form four ordinary words.

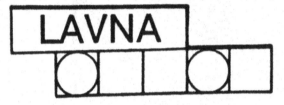

LAVNA

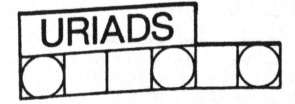

YATTS

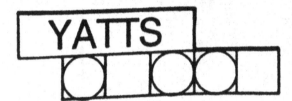

MAGITS

URIADS

Looks like gridlock

THE REGATTA WAS SO FULL OF SAILBOATS THAT IT MADE ONE THINK OF THIS.

Now arrange the circled letters to form the surprise answer, as suggested by the above cartoon.

Answer: "⬡⬡⬡⬡" ⬡⬡⬡⬡⬡⬡⬡⬡

# JUMBLE.

Unscramble these four Jumbles, one letter to each square, to form four ordinary words.

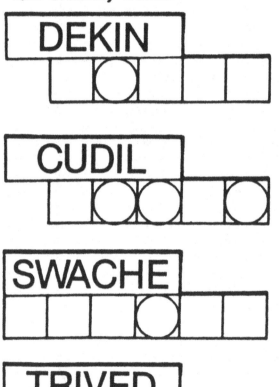

DEKIN

CUDIL

SWACHE

TRIVED

WHAT THOSE TOURISTS GOT WHILE IN HOLLAND.

Now arrange the circled letters to form the surprise answer, as suggested by the above cartoon.

Print answer here:

# JUMBLE®

Unscramble these four Jumbles, one letter to each square, to form four ordinary words.

DOITI

THERB

PHILSO

BASHUM

Wait' I you hear this...

Wait'll YOU hear THIS!!!

WHEN NEIGHBORS GOSSIP OVER A FENCE, THERE'S MUCH TO BE SAID---

Now arrange the circled letters to form the surprise answer, as suggested by the above cartoon.

Answer here:  ON ⬡⬡⬡⬡  ⬡⬡⬡⬡⬡

116

# JUMBLE.

Unscramble these four Jumbles,
one letter to each square, to form
four ordinary words.

ODARR

VIRTE

SUNGUF

FORFET

Looks like he's hit
everyone here today

WHAT IT TAKES
FOR A DEADBEAT
TO KEEP AFLOAT.

Now arrange the circled letters to
form the surprise answer, as suggested by the above cartoon.

Answer: A ☐☐☐☐☐ OF ☐☐☐☐☐☐☐

▽△▽△▽△▽△▽△▽△▽△▽△▽△▽△▽△▽△▽△▽△▽

# JUMBLE.

Unscramble these four Jumbles,
one letter to each square, to form
four ordinary words.

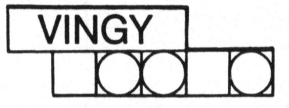

VINGY

ENDOM

FARITY

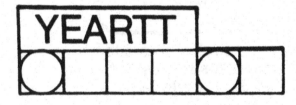

YEARTT

He must learn to save
part of his allowance

THAT SPOILED KID
WOULD RATHER
CRY AND GET
IT THAN---

Now arrange the circled letters to
form the surprise answer, as suggested by the above cartoon.

Answer here:  ◯◯◯ AND ◯◯◯◯ ◯◯

118

# JUMBLE.

Unscramble these four Jumbles,
one letter to each square, to form
four ordinary words.

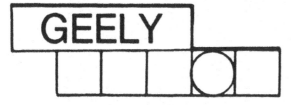

GEELY

ACNIP

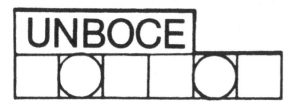

UNBOCE

CAFRIB

ANOTHER NAME FOR
ALL THAT BAGGAGE
THAT GOES INTO
THE VEHICLE.

Now arrange the circled letters to
form the surprise answer, as suggested by the above cartoon.

Print answer here:

▲▼▲▼▲▼▲▼▲▼▲▼▲▼▲▼▲▼▲▼▲▼▲▼▲▼▲▼▲

# JUMBLE®

Unscramble these four Jumbles,
one letter to each square, to form
four ordinary words.

**MOPET**

**DOBOL**

**VARMEL**

**PRIMEE**

That'll make
the property
nicer

WHAT A SKILLED
GARDENER KNOWS
HOW TO DO.

Now arrange the circled letters to
form the surprise answer, as suggested by the above cartoon.

Answer: ☐☐☐☐☐☐☐ HIS " ☐☐☐ "

# JUMBLE.

Unscramble these four Jumbles,
one letter to each square, to form
four ordinary words.

NATEC

YUCIJ

CORCUN

POITTE

WHAT A PICNIC
WITH KIDS
SOMETIMES IS.

Now arrange the circled letters to
form the surprise answer, as suggested by the above cartoon.

*Print answer here:* "  "

# JUMBLE®

Unscramble these four Jumbles, one letter to each square, to form four ordinary words.

KADEB

TAFOO

RUMIAD

NIMERV

WHAT THE SAILOR SHOUTED WHEN HE SAW THE SURFER.

Now arrange the circled letters to form the surprise answer, as suggested by the above cartoon.

Answer: ⬡⬡⬡ " ⬡⬡⬡⬡⬡ ⬡⬡⬡⬡⬡ "

# JUMBLE®

Unscramble these four Jumbles, one letter to each square, to form four ordinary words.

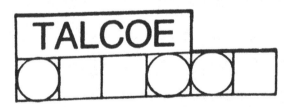

BEATA

KERPI

RUTTEL

TALCOE

Let me tell you what that couple did

IF YOU'RE CONCERNED ABOUT RATTLESNAKES, START RUNNING WHEN YOU HEAR THIS.

Now arrange the circled letters to form the surprise answer, as suggested by the above cartoon.

Answer: A [ ][ ][ ][ ][ ][ ] " [ ][ ][ ][ ] "

# JUMBLE®

Unscramble these four Jumbles,
one letter to each square, to form
four ordinary words.

RETEB

VENIA

GETMAN

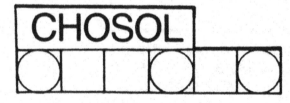

CHOSOL

WHAT THE LION
TAMER WOULD HAVE
PREFERRED.

Now arrange the circled letters to
form the surprise answer, as suggested by the above cartoon.

Answer here:

# JUMBLE®

Unscramble these four Jumbles,
one letter to each square, to form
four ordinary words.

**YOSIN**

**CAINB**

**DASSIT**

**RASHEE**

FOR A MOTHER ---

Now arrange the circled letters to
form the surprise answer, as suggested by the above cartoon.

Answer: THE ◯◯◯ ALWAYS ◯◯◯◯◯◯

▲▼▲▼▲▼▲▼▲▼▲▼▲▼▲▼▲▼▲▼▲▼▲▼▲▼▲

# JUMBLE®

Unscramble these four Jumbles,
one letter to each square, to form
four ordinary words.

HOLEL

KARNC

NITTEY

LAWESE

IN HER BATHING
SUIT, SHE REVEALED
LEGS THAT
WERE THIS.

Now arrange the circled letters to
form the surprise answer, as suggested by the above cartoon.

Answer here: "◯◯◯◯◯◯◯◯◯"

126

# JUMBLE.

Unscramble these four Jumbles,
one letter to each square, to form
four ordinary words.

LEVOG

ZARCY

NETTAX

CRONAR

THERE ARE SOME
WHO SAY THIS IS
THE BEST BUTTER.

Now arrange the circled letters to
form the surprise answer, as suggested by the above cartoon.

*Print answer here:*

# JUMBLE.

Unscramble these four Jumbles,
one letter to each square, to form
four ordinary words.

MERIC

ALQUI

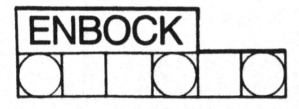

ENBOCK

CHECIT

NEVER HAVE SO
MANY OWED SO
MUCH TO SO
LITTLE ---

Now arrange the circled letters to
form the surprise answer, as suggested by the above cartoon.

Print answer here:

128

# JUMBLE.

Unscramble these four Jumbles,
one letter to each square, to form
four ordinary words.

TOINX

EBILE

YALDDE

LUMUTT

THE MOON
AFFECTS THIS.

Now arrange the circled letters to
form the surprise answer, as suggested by the above cartoon.

Answer: THE ⬡⬡⬡⬡ AND THE ⬡⬡⬡⬡⬡⬡

# JUMBLE.

Unscramble these four Jumbles, one letter to each square, to form four ordinary words.

FELKA

AMMIX

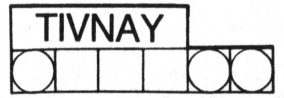

TIVNAY

HARANG

He won by a tremendous margin and look at him now

IN POLITICS THIS IS WHERE THE "PATHS OF GLORY" MIGHT LEAD.

Now arrange the circled letters to form the surprise answer, as suggested by the above cartoon.

Answer here: TO ⬡⬡⬡ " ⬡⬡⬡⬡⬡ "

# JUMBLE®

Unscramble these four Jumbles, one letter to each square, to form four ordinary words.

WROPE

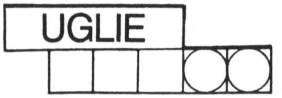

UGLIE

LYNFOD

MIRSUQ

THE HARDEST THING TO RAISE IN A GARDEN.

Now arrange the circled letters to form the surprise answer, as suggested by the above cartoon.

Print answer here:

# JUMBLE®

Unscramble these four Jumbles, one letter to each square, to form four ordinary words.

BROIN

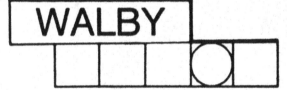

WALBY

TEVVLE

CUSSEN

A LEASH IS A LINE BY WHICH A DOG IS HELD IN CHECK BY A PERSON----

Now arrange the circled letters to form the surprise answer, as suggested by the above cartoon.

Answer here: OR ⬡⬡⬡⬡⬡ ⬡⬡⬡⬡⬡

# JUMBLE.

Unscramble these four Jumbles,
one letter to each square, to form
four ordinary words.

KANTE

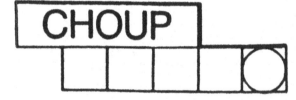

CHOUP

RASTUX

PHEPOR

WHAT A BATHING
SUIT DEVELOPS
AFTER IT'S PUT ON.

Now arrange the circled letters to
form the surprise answer, as suggested by the above cartoon.

Print answer here:

# JUMBLE.

Unscramble these four Jumbles, one letter to each square, to form four ordinary words.

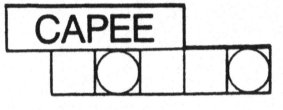

CAPEE

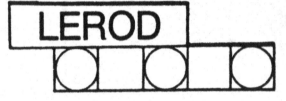

LEROD

MEAFED

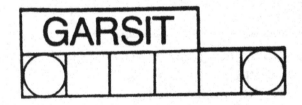

GARSIT

Now it's up to you —

WILL A COLLEGE EDUCATION HELP HIM TO SUCCEED IN LIFE?

Now arrange the circled letters to form the surprise answer, as suggested by the above cartoon.

Answer: TO ◯◯◯◯◯ " ◯◯◯◯◯◯◯ "

134

# JUMBLE®

Unscramble these four Jumbles,
one letter to each square, to form
four ordinary words.

ORRGI

HOBAR

DELIRB

KATINE

WHAT THEY CALLED
THAT DAFT
ORNITHOLOGIST.

Now arrange the circled letters to
form the surprise answer, as suggested by the above cartoon.

Answer here: "◯◯◯◯◯◯◯◯◯"

▲▼▲▼▲▼▲▼▲▼▲▼▲▼▲▼▲▼▲▼▲▼▲▼▲▼▲

# JUMBLE®

Unscramble these four Jumbles, one letter to each square, to form four ordinary words.

YEGEL

BLOIM

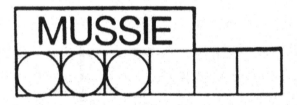

MUSSIE

PREMAT

COULD BE THE GOOD OLD SUMMERTIME.

Now arrange the circled letters to form the surprise answer, as suggested by the above cartoon.

Answer here: " ⬡⬡⬡⬡⬡⬡ ⬡⬡⬡⬡ "

# JUMBLE.

Unscramble these four Jumbles, one letter to each square, to form four ordinary words.

DIELY

GYROL

TELKIN

HUNOLY

A BACHELOR IS A MAN WHO CAN GO FISHING ANYTIME---

Now arrange the circled letters to form the surprise answer, as suggested by the above cartoon.

Answer: [ ] [ ] [ ] [ ] HE GETS " [ ] [ ] [ ] [ ] [ ] [ ] "

▲▼▲▼▲▼▲▼▲▼▲▼▲▼▲▼▲▼▲▼▲▼▲▼▲▼▲▼▲▼

# JUMBLE.

Unscramble these four Jumbles,
one letter to each square, to form
four ordinary words.

**RYHUR**

**FOOLI**

**NECNAD**

**UPCATE**

THE GARDENER
FOUND THAT TOPSOIL
IS NO LONGER THIS.

Now arrange the circled letters to
form the surprise answer, as suggested by the above cartoon.

*Answer here:* "◯◯◯◯" ◯◯◯◯◯◯

# JUMBLE.

Unscramble these four Jumbles,
one letter to each square, to form
four ordinary words.

CASHO

DALIP

KABETS

URAMAD

IT WAS SO HOT,
THE THERMOMETER
WAS THIS.

Now arrange the circled letters to
form the surprise answer, as suggested by the above cartoon.

Answer here: ⬡⬡ IN THE " ⬡⬡⬡⬡⬡ "

139

# JUMBLE®

Unscramble these four Jumbles,
one letter to each square, to form
four ordinary words.

PODOR

HOACC

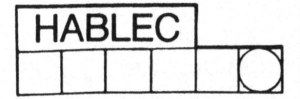

HABLEC

TORRCE

WHAT THE BIRD WAS
LOOKING FOR WHEN
HE FLEW OVER
ALL THOSE FISH.

Now arrange the circled letters to
form the surprise answer, as suggested by the above cartoon.

Print answer here:

# JUMBLE.

Unscramble these four Jumbles,
one letter to each square, to form
four ordinary words.

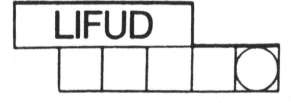

LIFUD

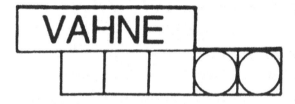

VAHNE

SUCLEM

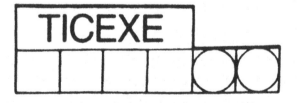

TICEXE

WHY THE
CONTORTIONIST
COMBED HIS HAIR
WITH HIS TOES.

Now arrange the circled letters to
form the surprise answer, as suggested by the above cartoon.

Answer here:  TO MAKE

# JUMBLE®

Unscramble these four Jumbles,
one letter to each square, to form
four ordinary words.

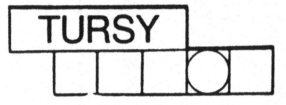

TURSY

EVERF

COAZID

ZYNEEM

WHERE THAT
ECCENTRIC
DANCER WENT.

Now arrange the circled letters to
form the surprise answer, as suggested by the above cartoon.

Answer: ⬡⬡⬡⬡⬡ WITH THE "⬡⬡⬡⬡"

# JUMBLE.

Unscramble these four Jumbles,
one letter to each square, to form
four ordinary words.

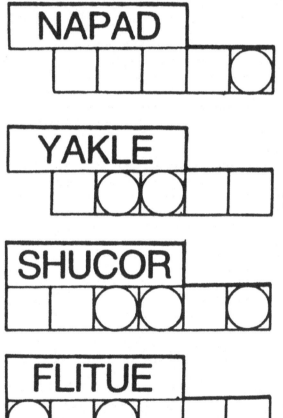

NAPAD

YAKLE

SHUCOR

FLITUE

Beats
walking
any day

THESE WORDS CAME
TO MIND WHEN HE
SAW THAT GLIDER
PILOT.

Now arrange the circled letters to
form the surprise answer, as suggested by the above cartoon.

Answer here: "☐☐☐☐" "☐☐☐☐"

# JUMBLE.

Unscramble these four Jumbles, one letter to each square, to form four ordinary words.

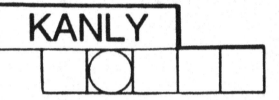

KANLY

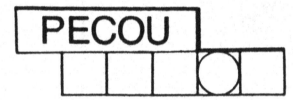

PECOU

CENTED

INVOCE

ANOTHER THING A YOUNG MOTHER SHOULD SAVE FOR A RAINY DAY.

Now arrange the circled letters to form the surprise answer, as suggested by the above cartoon.

Print answer here:

144

# JUMBLE.

Unscramble these four Jumbles,
one letter to each square, to form
four ordinary words.

ONLOY

MYLOD

BAACAN

KLEETT

WHERE CAN YOU
FIND A GOOD
CARD GAME ON
A BIG SHIP?

Now arrange the circled letters to
form the surprise answer, as suggested by the above cartoon.

Print answer here: ◯◯◯ " ◯◯◯◯ "

# JUMBLE.

Unscramble these four Jumbles,
one letter to each square, to form
four ordinary words.

DARNB

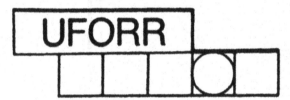

UFORR

CATHED

LAUTES

WHAT THE FARMER
HAD THAT MADE
THE COW JUMP
OVER THE MOON.

Now arrange the circled letters to
form the surprise answer, as suggested by the above cartoon.

Print answer here:

146

# JUMBLE.

Unscramble these four Jumbles, one letter to each square, to form four ordinary words.

**CUIJE**

**SAYTH**

**PITTYS**

**INTYCE**

WHAT THEY EXPECTED THE BALL-PLAYER TO DO WHEN HE JOINED THEIR CAMPING PARTY.

Now arrange the circled letters to form the surprise answer, as suggested by the above cartoon.

Answer: " ☐☐☐☐☐☐ " THE ☐☐☐☐

147

▲▼▲▼▲▼▲▼▲▼▲▼▲▼▲▼▲▼▲▼▲▼▲▼▲▼▲▼▲▼

# JUMBLE.

Unscramble these four Jumbles, one letter to each square, to form four ordinary words.

VEYON

ZYIZD

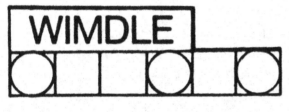

WIMDLE

ENICKS

THE ONLY PEOPLE WHO WERE SAFE WHEN THAT MAN-EATING TIGER GOT LOOSE.

Now arrange the circled letters to form the surprise answer, as suggested by the above cartoon.

Answer here: ⬡⬡⬡⬡⬡ & ⬡⬡⬡⬡

# JUMBLE.

Unscramble these four Jumbles, one letter to each square, to form four ordinary words.

YONEH

DIGUE

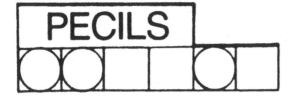

PECILS

LASTOP

RESPONSIBLE FOR THAT HOLDUP IN THE BACK YARD.

Now arrange the circled letters to form the surprise answer, as suggested by the above cartoon.

Answer here: ◯◯◯◯◯◯◯◯◯◯◯◯◯

# JUMBLE®

Unscramble these four Jumbles,
one letter to each square, to form
four ordinary words.

WEPOR

LOVEN

NYGERT

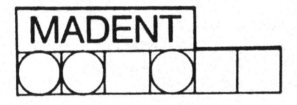

MADENT

CANINE COLLEGE

THEIR FAMILY PET
WAS SO BRIGHT
THAT HE EARNED
THIS.

Now arrange the circled letters to
form the surprise answer, as suggested by the above cartoon.

Answer: HIS "◯◯◯ - ◯◯◯◯◯◯◯"

# JUMBLE.

Unscramble these four Jumbles, one letter to each square, to form four ordinary words.

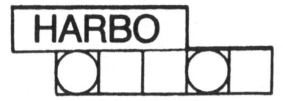

**HARBO**

**DOLOB**

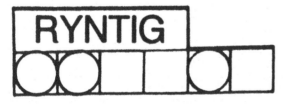

**MELBUH**

**RYNTIG**

YOUR FAMILY WASH IN THE BACKYARD?

Now arrange the circled letters to form the surprise answer, as suggested by the above cartoon.

Answer: " ⬜⬜⬜ , THE ⬜⬜⬜⬜⬜⬜⬜⬜⬜ "

151

▲▼▲▼▲▼▲▼▲▼▲▼▲▼▲▼▲▼▲▼▲▼▲▼▲▼▲▼▲▼▲▼▲▼▲

# JUMBLE®

Unscramble these four Jumbles,
one letter to each square, to form
four ordinary words.

**KANEL**

**CROAG**

**REWEPT**

**GANNIA**

They're coming
your way

HOW THE FISHING
FLEET CAUGHT ITS
DAILY LIMIT.

Now arrange the circled letters to
form the surprise answer, as suggested by the above cartoon.

Answer: BY " ⬡⬡⬡ " – ⬡⬡⬡⬡⬡⬡⬡⬡

# JUMBLE®

Unscramble these four Jumbles,
one letter to each square, to form
four ordinary words.

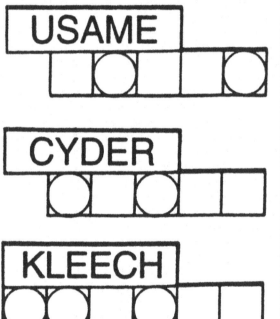

USAME

CYDER

KLEECH

BIRDHY

What are you doing here?

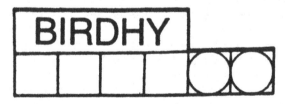

WHAT THE GUARD
DID TO THE
SHIP'S INTRUDER.

Now arrange the circled letters to
form the surprise answer, as suggested by the above cartoon.

Answer here: HE

# JUMBLE.

Unscramble these four Jumbles,
one letter to each square, to form
four ordinary words.

ALIVA

NACYF

BOULED

CATLEK

Your check bounced

THE TIGHTROPE
WALKER GOT INTO
TROUBLE BECAUSE
HE HAD A----

Now arrange the circled letters to
form the surprise answer, as suggested by the above cartoon.

Answer: ⬡⬡⬡⬡ OF ⬡⬡⬡⬡⬡⬡⬡⬡

# JUMBLE®

Unscramble these four Jumbles,
one letter to each square, to form
four ordinary words.

**TOIDI**

**SNAIB**

**SPOCER**

**BILBEN**

This is a kind of
sea animal

HOW THE
VISITORS REACTED TO
THE SPONGE DIVER'S
LECTURE.

Now arrange the circled letters to
form the surprise answer, as suggested by the above cartoon.

*Answer here:* THEY
WERE

155

▲▼▲▼▲▼▲▼▲▼▲▼▲▼▲▼▲▼▲▼▲▼▲▼▲▼▲▼▲▼▲▼▲▼▲

# JUMBLE®

Unscramble these four Jumbles,
one letter to each square, to form
four ordinary words.

WYLEN

KOSMY

VACTAR

TUGIRA

They're everywhere

WHAT THEY BECAME
WHEN THE INSECTS
ATTACKED.

Now arrange the circled letters to
form the surprise answer, as suggested by the above cartoon.

*Print answer here:* THE ⬡⬡⬡⬡ ⬡⬡⬡⬡

▲▼▲▼▲▼▲▼▲▼▲▼▲▼▲▼▲▼▲▼▲▼▲▼▲▼▲

# JUMBLE®

Unscramble these four Jumbles,
one letter to each square, to form
four ordinary words.

**CHAVO**

**DREEL**

**ERRTAY**

**BLUHME**

How does he do that?

THE KIND OF LIFE
SOME SNAKES LEAD.

Now arrange the circled letters to
form the surprise answer, as suggested by the above cartoon.

Print answer here:

157

# JUMBLE®

Unscramble these four Jumbles,
one letter to each square, to form
four ordinary words.

KLEAF

GELEY

RALCOR

TURIAL

They sing so
beautifully

WHAT THE
BIRDS GAVE THE
NATURE LOVERS.

Now arrange the circled letters to
form the surprise answer, as suggested by the above cartoon.

Answer here:  A ⬡⬡⬡⬡⬡ ⬡⬡⬡⬡⬡

# JUMBLE.

Unscramble these four Jumbles,
one letter to each square, to form
four ordinary words.

DRATY

VOYIR

TALKEN

MILTEY

'Bye, Grandma

WHAT SOME
LEAVE BEHIND
WHEN GETTING AWAY
FROM IT ALL.

Now arrange the circled letters to
form the surprise answer, as suggested by the above cartoon.

Answer here:

159

# JUMBLE.

Unscramble these four Jumbles,
one letter to each square, to form
four ordinary words.

LITRL

DUXEE

DARFIA

BILDOY

So THAT'S who he's
been dating!

WHAT THE LANDSCAPER
UNCOVERED IN THE
ROYAL GARDEN.

Now arrange the circled letters to
form the surprise answer, as suggested by the above cartoon.

*Print answer here:* THE ☐☐☐☐ ☐☐☐☐

# JUMBLE.

Unscramble these four Jumbles, one letter to each square, to form four ordinary words.

INBAC

TUCOL

REECCO

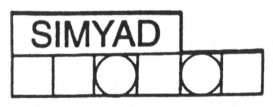
SIMYAD

BANK

Now we can get a tan in the sun

WHY THE BANK ROBBERS HEADED FOR THE SEASHORE.

Now arrange the circled letters to form the surprise answer, as suggested by the above cartoon.

Answer: THE ⬡⬡⬡⬡⬡ WAS ⬡⬡⬡⬡⬡

▲▽▲▽▲▽▲▽▲▽▲▽▲▽▲▽▲▽▲▽▲▽▲▽▲▽▲▽▲▽▲

# JUMBLE®

Unscramble these four Jumbles,
one letter to each square, to form
four ordinary words.

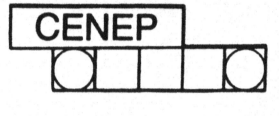

CENEP

CAGIM

SIBULY

ERIFEC

I'm marking it
down for cash

WHAT HE OFFERED THE
PROSPECTIVE BUYER.

Now arrange the circled letters to
form the surprise answer, as suggested by the above cartoon.

Answer here: A "⬡⬡⬡⬡⬡" ⬡⬡⬡⬡⬡⬡

# JUMBLE®

Unscramble these four Jumbles,
one letter to each square, to form
four ordinary words.

SERCS

WROPE

FAINAR

GOURAC

That looks like a good spot

Gosh--I don't know

!?!?

WHY THE PILOT
COULDN'T DECIDE
WHERE TO LAND.

Now arrange the circled letters to
form the surprise answer, as suggested by the above cartoon.

Answer here: HE ⬭⬭⬭ ⬭⬭ IN THE ⬭⬭⬭

# JUMBLE®

Unscramble these four Jumbles, one letter to each square, to form four ordinary words.

LUGIE

TRAFE

DUBUSE

GLEGGI

Next she'll get her doctorate

HOW SHE IMPROVED HER KNOWLEDGE.

Now arrange the circled letters to form the surprise answer, as suggested by the above cartoon.

Print answer here: BY ☐☐☐☐☐☐☐

164

# JUMBLE®

Unscramble these four Jumbles,
one letter to each square, to form
four ordinary words.

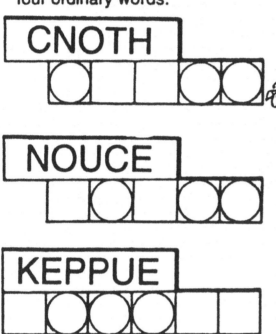

**CNOTH**

**NOUCE**

**KEPPUE**

**ICKEOO**

WHAT THE POULTRY
FARMER CALLED THE
CAR HE DROVE
TO MARKET.

Now arrange the circled letters to
form the surprise answer, as suggested by the above cartoon.

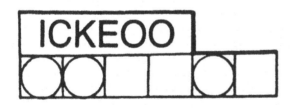

**Answer:** HIS ◯◯◯◯◯◯◯ ◯◯◯◯◯

# JUMBLE®

Unscramble these four Jumbles,
one letter to each square, to form
four ordinary words.

UGGEA

SNAIE

OETAGE

RETHEN

It'll be the
making of us

HOW THE
CHICKEN FARMER
GOT HIS START.

Now arrange the circled letters to
form the surprise answer, as suggested by the above cartoon.

Print answer here: WITH A

# JUMBLE®

Unscramble these four Jumbles,
one letter to each square, to form
four ordinary words.

**WOALG**

**TUFIR**

**BONGEY**

**SERBIC**

Stay under the umbrella

WHAT HE
DID WHEN SHE
FORGOT THE SUN
BLOCK LOTION.

Now arrange the circled letters to
form the surprise answer, as suggested by the above cartoon.

*Print answer here:* A

▲▼▲▼▲▼▲▼▲▼▲▼▲▼▲▼▲▼▲▼▲▼▲▼▲▼▲▼▲▼

# JUMBLE®

Unscramble these four Jumbles,
one letter to each square, to form
four ordinary words.

INVEA

TALAN

HALIDA

SHORKE

No ringing, no
busy signals

WHAT THE PHONE
OPERATOR LIKED TO
DO ON VACATION.

Now arrange the circled letters to
form the surprise answer, as suggested by the above cartoon.

Answer:

# JUMBLE®

Unscramble these four Jumbles,
one letter to each square, to form
four ordinary words.

TRAAL

DULIF

SUMMUE

ZEEWEH

Try one—I made this
batch yesterday

WHAT THE WELL-
TO-DO CANDY
MAKER ENJOYED.

Now arrange the circled letters to
form the surprise answer, as suggested by the above cartoon.

Answer here: THE ⬡⬡⬡⬡⬡ ⬡⬡⬡⬡

169

# JUMBLE®

Unscramble these four Jumbles,
one letter to each square, to form
four ordinary words.

BAYBE

ROCKA

CHEROM

DETHOB

EAUTY PARLOR

WHAT THE
HAIR STYLIST
AT THE SEASHORE
WAS CALLED.

Now arrange the circled letters to
form the surprise answer, as suggested by the above cartoon.

Answer: A ☐☐☐☐☐ ☐☐☐☐☐☐

170

# CHALLENGER

## SUMMER FUN
## JUMBLE®

▲▼▲▼▲▼▲▼▲▼▲▼▲▼▲▼▲▼▲▼▲▼▲▼▲▼▲▼

# JUMBLE®

Unscramble these six Jumbles,
one letter to each square,
to form six ordinary words.

CASMIO

VONCLE

AGGIZZ

LUGGEJ

NAUCIV

VAQUER

Are they
wearing
anything
at all?

WHY MODERN SWIMSUITS
ARE REAL "COOL."

Now arrange the circled letters
to form the surprise answer, as
suggested by the above cartoon.

Print the SURPRISE
ANSWER here

THEY'RE ◯◯◯◯ "◯◯◯◯"

# JUMBLE®

Unscramble these six Jumbles,
one letter to each square,
to form six ordinary words.

**RIVACA**

**PANUCK**

**BALLEF**

**UMPAKE**

**SIXECE**

**ANQUIT**

Giddyap!!!

WHAT YOU GET
ON THIS FARM.

Now arrange the circled letters
to form the surprise answer, as
suggested by the above cartoon.

Print the SURPRISE
ANSWER here

◯◯◯◯◯◯◯◯◯ & ◯◯◯◯◯

▲▼▲▼▲▼▲▼▲▼▲▼▲▼▲▼▲▼▲▼▲▼▲▼▲▼▲▼▲▼

# JUMBLE®

Unscramble these six Jumbles,
one letter to each square,
to form six ordinary words.

**MUPTIE**

**PUNCOO**

**OCTIXE**

**SHOIBY**

**DUSARI**

**LOSTID**

WHAT YOU'LL FIND
PLENTY OF AT THE
BEACH ON SUNDAY.

Now arrange the circled letters
to form the surprise answer, as
suggested by the above cartoon.

Print the SURPRISE ANSWER here

# JUMBLE®

Unscramble these six Jumbles,
one letter to each square,
to form six ordinary words.

**INSORP**

**PERTIL**

**SAUTLE**

**VIKONE**

**IMVOTE**

**GLAITH**

Last one in is
a rotten egg!

HOW TO GET YOUR
CLOTHES OFF FASTER
THAN THE OTHERS.

Now arrange the circled letters
to form the surprise answer, as
suggested by the above cartoon.

Print the SURPRISE
ANSWER here

▲▼▲▼▲▼▲▼▲▼▲▼▲▼▲▼▲▼▲▼▲▼▲▼▲▼▲

# JUMBLE®

Unscramble these six Jumbles,
one letter to each square,
to form six ordinary words.

**TELRUT**

**NOCHOP**

**RENUNG**

**TEASET**

**WINDAR**

**DIASUN**

WHAT HAPPENED WHEN
THE GRAPES WERE
TRAMPLED ON.

Now arrange the circled letters
to form the surprise answer, as
suggested by the above cartoon.

ANSWER here **THEY** ☐☐☐☐ ☐☐☐☐ ☐ "☐☐☐☐"

# JUMBLE®

Unscramble these six Jumbles,
one letter to each square,
to form six ordinary words.

**INDATE**

**BOCIXE**

**GOAFER**

**ELBARR**

**CHOTLE**

**DELNAH**

Must be cold back home

WHAT HE SAID WHEN ASKED WHY HE STOLE A PURSE.

Now arrange the circled letters to form the surprise answer, as suggested by the above cartoon.

Print the ANSWER here I ⭕⭕⭕⭕⭕⭕ THE ⭕⭕⭕⭕⭕⭕

# JUMBLE®

Unscramble these six Jumbles,
one letter to each square,
to form six ordinary words.

**NABYRD**

**GAAMED**

**CLIPES**

**DULCOY**

**TANFIN**

**WEVILS**

Tonight I'm popping the question

WHAT HE HOPED
THE HULA DANCER
WOULD BE.

Now arrange the circled letters
to form the surprise answer, as
suggested by the above cartoon.

Print the SURPRISE ANSWER here

# JUMBLE®

Unscramble these six Jumbles,
one letter to each square,
to form six ordinary words.

**MACTIP**

**HESTOO**

**CAUTAL**

**TUITOW**

**RAHNGE**

**LUFOWE**

A SEE-THROUGH SHIRT
MIGHT BE SUITABLE
FOR A MAN WHO
HAS TO DO THIS.

Now arrange the circled letters
to form the surprise answer, as
suggested by the above cartoon.

ANSWER here 〇〇〇〇〇 **HIS** 〇〇〇〇〇〇〇〇〇〇

▲▼▲▼▲▼▲▼▲▼▲▼▲▼▲▼▲▼▲▼▲▼▲▼▲▼▲

# JUMBLE®

Unscramble these six Jumbles, one letter to each square, to form six ordinary words.

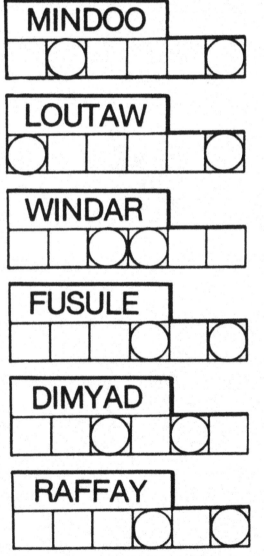

MINDOO

LOUTAW

WINDAR

FUSULE

DIMYAD

RAFFAY

That'll help you get a good job

WHAT A SHEEPSKIN IS INTENDED TO KEEP.

Now arrange the circled letters to form the surprise answer, as suggested by the above cartoon.

**PRINT YOUR ANSWER IN THE CIRCLES BELOW**

THE ◯◯◯◯◯ ◯◯◯◯◯ FROM THE ◯◯◯◯

# JUMBLE®

Unscramble these six Jumbles, one letter to each square, to form six ordinary words.

TELKIN

DEGAMA

CUPHIC

FRIDAT

GURMOE

SNOOPI

Careful!

WHAT YOU MIGHT END UP WITH IF YOU HAPPEN TO TOUCH POISON IVY WHILE PICKING A FOUR-LEAF CLOVER.

Now arrange the circled letters to form the surprise answer, as suggested by the above cartoon.

**PRINT YOUR ANSWER IN THE CIRCLES BELOW**

A " ⬡⬡⬡⬡ " OF ⬡⬡⬡⬡⬡ ⬡⬡⬡⬡

# JUMBLE.

Unscramble these six Jumbles,
one letter to each square, to form
six ordinary words.

SIMREY

FRILPE

ARUSSE

ENCHEW

TYRITH

ZANATS

WHAT AN OLDSTER
SOMETIMES
PREFERS.

Now arrange the circled letters to
form the surprise answer, as suggested by the above cartoon.

## PRINT YOUR ANSWER IN THE CIRCLES BELOW

A ☐☐☐☐☐☐ TO A ☐☐☐☐☐☐☐

# JUMBLE.

Unscramble these six Jumbles, one letter to each square, to form six ordinary words.

RAHGEC

LOWLAF

BURGYB

COZADI

YARROS

KLANTE

WHAT KIND OF A CHARACTER WAS THE GUY WHO WAS LYING UNDER A TREE WATCHING HIS WIFE MOW THE LAWN?

Now arrange the circled letters to form the surprise answer, as suggested by the above cartoon.

**PRINT YOUR ANSWER IN THE CIRCLES BELOW**

# JUMBLE.

Unscramble these six Jumbles, one letter to each square, to form six ordinary words.

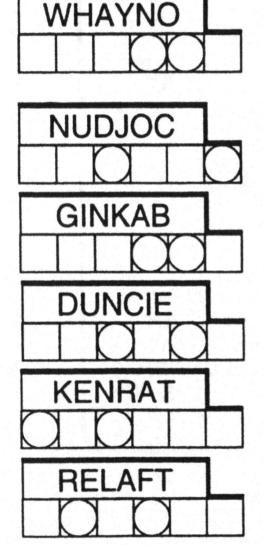

WHAYNO

NUDJOC

GINKAB

DUNCIE

KENRAT

RELAFT

Whoops

Don't call us--
We'll call you

WHY THE
APPRENTICE TRAPEZE
ARTIST COULDN'T
HOLD THE JOB.

Now arrange the circled letters to form the surprise answer, as suggested by the above cartoon.

**PRINT YOUR ANSWER IN THE CIRCLES BELOW**

HE ◯◯◯◯◯'◯ ◯◯◯◯◯◯ ◯◯

# ANSWERS

1. **Jumbles:** OLDER AHEAD HEREBY UNRULY
**Answer:** What they said when Venus of Milo came to dinner—YOU GOTTA HAND IT TO HER!

2. **Jumbles:** MAIZE SWOON BOTTLE PRAYER
**Answer:** What they might have at an Italian picnic—"ROME-ANTS"

3. **Jumbles:** AGING CHANT NEWEST ECZEMA
**Answer:** Where you might find good French soup—IN "CANNES"

4. **Jumbles:** CURVE VALET INVITE FELLOW
**Answer:** French toast—VIVE LA FRANCE

5. **Jumbles:** IDIOT NAVAL TAWDRY CANYON
**Answer:** What a thirsty man might do in Formosa—"TAIWAN" ON

6. **Jumbles:** LIMIT SCOUT BEDECK DREDGE
**Answer:** Why you should never let grass grow under your feet—IT TICKLES

7. **Jumbles:** ELOPE BIRCH HAUNCH GAINED
**Answer:** Fruit sometimes found in the sand—A BEACH PEACH

8. **Jumbles:** MILKY ESSAY PARLOR FOMENT
**Answer:** What people who don't summer in the country often do in the city—SIMMER

9. **Jumbles:** EJECT SAHIB KILLER BELONG
**Answer:** Some veteran gardeners might find this the hardest thing to raise—THEIR KNEES

10. **Jumbles:** MADLY OXIDE TURKEY BOILED
**Answer:** A ten-letter word that starts with G-A-S—AUTOMOBILE

11. **Jumbles:** TONIC LEGAL HELMET OPENLY
**Answer:** Many a guy has been stung trying to get this—A LITTLE HONEY

12. **Jumbles:** ROBIN FLUTE EMPIRE FOSSIL
**Answer:** Where you have mountain ranges you might also find this—FOREST FIRES

13. **Jumbles:** THINK FORAY SAFARI ACCESS
**Answer:** This might be conspicuous in some underwater play—A STARFISH

14. **Jumbles:** BULGY JUICE AERATE CODGER
**Answer:** What a bright gold digger's weapon might be—HER "EYE-CUE"

15. **Jumbles:** HARPY TAKEN MISERY FAIRLY
**Answer:** What the guy who claimed he could read women like a book must have been—A MYSTERY FAN

16. **Jumbles:** ASSAY MOTHY ZEALOT TYPING
**Answer:** What a baby might be in warm weather—A HOTSY TOTSY

17. **Jumbles:** DRYLY NOISE ALIGHT LICHEN
**Answer:** These kids might make THE RICH LEND—THE CHILDREN

18. **Jumbles:** VALOR FUDGE CARBON MEMOIR
**Answer:** When it's wet, get under it!—COVER

19. **Jumbles:** PANDA KITTY BEYOND GRISLY
**Answer:** What the pig said as the sun grew hotter—I'M BAKIN'

20. **Jumbles:** BERET OPERA ANEMIA PONCHO
**Answer:** The cheapest way to get to Europe—BE BORN THERE

21. **Jumbles:** DEITY ABYSS BEHELD PUSHER
**Answer:** At the bottom of successful gardening—SEEDS

22. **Jumbles:** ALIAS TROTH BUCKET COMEDY
**Answer:** What a boy who hates books might prefer to do—BAIT HOOKS

23. **Jumbles:** GUILT DEMON VERBAL PIRACY
**Answers:** How the road gang entertained the drivers—BY DIVERTING THEM

24. **Jumbles:** IGLOO VALOR MALLET ACHING
**Answer:** Why leaving your old home might be emotionally disturbing—IT'S "MOVING"

25. **Jumbles:** BANJO TYPED HANDLE FASTEN
**Answer:** They sometimes work around the clock on the farm—"HANDS"

26. **Jumbles:** NOVEL GRIPE ABSORB DAINTY
**Answer:** Provides the main course on board ship—THE NAVIGATOR

27. **Jumbles:** DAUNT CHAMP SUBMIT INVERT
**Answer:** Background material for an artist—CANVAS

28. **Jumbles:** MONEY BOUND FOMENT LADING
**Answer:** "Come out in the garden!"—"BLOOM"

29. **Jumbles:** PATCH SWISH MAGPIE JIGGER
**Answer:** Several in a flight—STEPS

30. **Jumbles:** STEED GAILY AMBUSH CALMLY
**Answer:** Might be barred in some parks—CAGES

31. **Jumbles:** OBESE PIECE TRIPLE FALLEN
**Answer:** An edible part of poppies that many become addicted to—"PIES"

32. **Jumbles:** TRYST SINGE BLOUSE MATURE
**Answer:** One who won't stand for being painted—A SITTER

33. **Jumbles:** CEASE AGATE CAMPUS DRIVEL
**Answer:** Could be the price of hiring a private guide to take you mountain climbing—STEEP

34. **Jumbles:** CRAZE DOGMA BANANA WAITER
**Answer:** What the desert rat said to his pal—WATER WE GONNA DO?

35. **Jumbles:** GORGE MINUS DELUXE IMPACT
**Answer:** How witch doctors keep fit—THEY "EXORCISE"

36. **Jumbles:** TEPID CHAFF BEHAVE GHETTO
**Answer:** What the proud giraffe kept—HER HEAD HIGH

37. **Jumbles:** OWING EMERY AMAZON FORBID
**Answer:** What you might find in Borneo—on a native—"NO ROBE"

38. **Jumbles:** FORTY ETUDE DRAGON GOVERN
**Answer:** What he said when asked whether he liked college—TO A "DEGREE"

39. **Jumbles:** GULCH ROUSE PALATE GIBBET
**Answer:** What bathing girls might be—"IN SLIGHT GARB"

40. **Jumbles:** HUMID GLOVE EXOTIC PIGEON
**Answer:** What "tequila" is—THE "GULP" OF MEXICO

41. **Jumbles:** SNOWY EXTOL PEPTIC MALADY
**Answer:** One paw of a big lion could be a dangerous one—"WEAPON"

42. **Jumbles:** CHESS CRAFT MORBID GRAVEN
**Answer:** Threatened to rain over the actors at the outdoor theater—"OVER CAST"

43. **Jumbles:** EXULT BRAVO UNSAID SEETHE
**Answer:** "You and I and no one else!"—OURSELVES

44. **Jumbles:** BUSHY DRYLY AGHAST FABLED
**Answer:** What you would expect to find plenty of in a military band composed mainly of officers—"BRASS"

45. **Jumbles:** SKIMP BRINY CONVEX HAUNCH
**Answer:** What time and grime do—RHYME

46. **Jumbles:** BAKED ADAPT WEDGED GARISH
**Answer:** What "changed" when the snow melted?—"THAW"

47. **Jumbles:** MERGE HONOR MILDEW BLOUSE
**Answer:** What word is it from which the whole may be taken, and yet some will be left?—"WHOLESOME"

48. **Jumbles:** MURKY BELIE NOODLE INDOOR
**Answer:** The egotist's favorite figure—NUMBER ONE

49. **Jumbles:** CROAK BAKED DAMAGE JOCUND
**Answer:** Cracked when it's heard—A JOKE

50. **Jumbles:** BULGY TRYST DOUBLE FEMALE
**Answer:** How to relax completely—"REST-FULLY"

51. **Jumbles:** SHYLY GUEST BEADLE KOSHER
**Answer:** They should improve the view—GLASSES

52. **Jumbles:** ENEMY AZURE BONNET COBALT
**Answer:** Sounds like a good hiding place—A TANNERY

53. **Jumbles:** PILOT GUMBO INVADE SINGLE
**Answer:** Sounded like some old-fashioned necking that might have caused a "stir"—"SPOONING"

54. **Jumbles:** HENNA UNCAP BUCKLE CHISEL
**Answer:** What the bathing beauty was—A BEACH PEACH

55. **Jumbles:** YEARN BASIN NEARLY ADJUST
**Answer:** If today's Jumble seems difficult, save it for this—A "BRAINY" DAY

56. **Jumbles:** BLOAT LINEN ABSURD HOMING
**Answer:** Goes up after a period of inflation—A BALLOON

57. **Jumbles:** PRUNE RIVET DEMISE HANGER
**Answer:** Really goes against the farmer's grain—HIS REAPER

58. **Jumbles:** POKER CURVE SHANTY FOIBLE
**Answer:** Little Bo-Peep lost her sheep because she had this—A "CROOK" WITH HER

59. **Jumbles:** DUMPY RABBI AERATE DRUDGE
**Answer:** It's good-by to a girl in Paris—"ADIEU"

60. **Jumbles:** BEFOG MOSSY AUTHOR MODERN
**Answer:** They provide a means of support for those who raise flowers—STEMS

61. **Jumbles:** USURY HITCH BROOCH ELIXIR
**Answer:** What the painter gave him—THE "BRUSH"

62. **Jumbles:** BRIBE SYNOD FAMOUS PREFER
**Answer:** What he said when inflation threatened to wipe out his nest egg—IT'S FOR THE BIRDS!

63. **Jumbles:** IGLOO FLOUT GIMLET BEHALF
**Answer:** What the baby bird expects mama to do at dinnertime—FILL THE BILL

64. **Jumbles:** ARBOR DUSKY FACADE HELMET
**Answer:** How the milking contest ended up—IN "UDDER" CHAOS

65. **Jumbles:** CRIME MOGUL QUORUM BANISH
**Answer:** In which it's difficult to row—when you "manipulate" huge oars—A "ROUGH SEA"

66. **Jumbles:** ENEMY MADAM GUILTY SECEDE
**Answer:** The best line to hook a woman with—"MASCU-LINE"

67. **Jumbles:** ERUPT FLOOR DELUXE GEYSER
**Answer:** At the seashore, your composure is often distracted by this—EXPOSURE

68. **Jumbles:** FORCE HUMID TOWARD NEPHEW
**Answer:** What a sudden cloudburst is—A "DROWN" POUR

69. **Jumbles:** PENCE OCTET HAZING CROUCH
**Answer:** Fishing may be a "disease," but it's not necessarily this—"CATCHING"

70. **Jumbles:** PAYEE WAFER BLITHE QUAVER
**Answer:** Why she dived into the sea—TO GET A WAVE IN HER HAIR

71. **Jumbles:** BELIE TRULY HAWKER LEVITY
**Answer:** Some people who think they're "in the swim" are just this—ALL WET

72. **Jumbles:** OZONE LLAMA PUNDIT QUEASY
**Answer:** Loves skin diving—A MOSQUITO

73. **Jumbles:** SUITE HASTY MARKUP STIGMA
**Answer:** What a hula dance is—A SHAKE IN THE GRASS

74. **Jumbles:** TITLE RIGOR GIMLET WINNOW
**Answer:** What happened to the bell that fell into the water?—IT WAS "RINGING" WET

75. **Jumbles:** APRON HANDY ENZYME BAZAAR
**Answer:** What the picnickers were—"HAMPERED"

76. **Jumbles:** ICILY CRACK MADMAN GYRATE
**Answer:** When they took that tropical vacation, they apparently were saving their money for this—A RAINY DAY

77. **Jumbles:** NOISY GNOME SUBWAY KETTLE
**Answer:** Even more fun than having a vacation is having this—THE BOSS TAKE ONE

78. **Jumbles:** BEGOT PUDGY TYPHUS CONCUR
**Answer:** What the pooped kangaroo was—"OUT OF BOUNDS"

79. **Jumbles:** EAGLE GASSY KITTEN MYSTIC
**Answer:** What the long tour made him—"SEE" SICK

80. **Jumbles:** DICED TYPED EQUATE PARITY
**Answer:** What's the problem with short skirts?—THE "UPCREEP"

81. **Jumbles:** SAVOR WRATH FELLOW EXEMPT
**Answer:** What his neighbor said when he showed off his new lawn equipment—"MOWER" POWER TO YOU

82. **Jumbles:** LIBEL CANAL BEHOLD DAWNED
**Answer:** What the rabbits who were playing in the onion patch had—A "BAWL"

83. **Jumbles:** COLIC QUOTA OUTLAW FLURRY
**Answer:** The gondolier may be serenading you, but he's ready for this—A "ROW"

84. **Jumbles:** IGLOO CHAOS GARLIC BARREN
**Answer:** What kind of a place was that rabbit farm?—"HARE-RAISING"

85. **Jumbles:** WEIGH BOWER BEHEAD CORRAL
**Answer:** What one bird said to the other—"WIRE WE HERE?"

86. **Jumbles:** GUISE JINGO MEDLEY UNLIKE
**Answer:** There was plenty of this when a quarrel broke out in the pigpen—MUDSLINGING

87. **Jumbles:** SCARF JEWEL WIZARD BUCKET
**Answer:** If a hungry shark is in the neighborhood, feed him this—JAWBREAKERS

88. **Jumbles:** TRACT LLAMA SCENIC TRUSTY
**Answer:** What those old sailing vessels must have provided—MAST TRANSIT

89. **Jumbles:** OAKEN ABATE PICNIC HOTBED
**Answer:** Where the stern captain always stood, naturally—AT THE BACK OF THE BOAT

90. **Jumbles:** TOXIN BLOOM REVERE LAUNCH
**Answer:** It's sometimes a crime to catch fish here, but more often this—A MIRACLE

91. **Jumbles:** CHAMP ROUSE HITHER FUMBLE
**Answer:** Snacks meant to refresh often end up doing this—"REFLESH"

92. **Jumbles:** RAVEN MOCHA INFECT OPPOSE
**Answer:** "Can you tell me what Napoleon's origin was?—"OF CORS-I-CAN"

93. **Jumbles:** GUMMY SURLY HEALTH GOVERN
**Answer:** The "one that got away" would have been bigger if the fisherman had this—LONGER ARMS

94. **Jumbles:** FAINT DICED INFIRM JESTER
**Answer:** What a sponger needs in order to keep afloat—A RAFT OF FRIENDS

95. **Jumbles:** KEYED WINCE INVITE BICEPS
**Answer:** What kind of game is croquet?—A "WICKET" ONE

96. **Jumbles:** QUASH ARBOR GAIETY CLOTHE
**Answer:** What the zookeeper said his life was—"BEASTLY"

97. **Jumbles:** KHAKI HARPY QUEASY TUMULT
**Answer:** What a belly laugh is—A "MIRTH" QUAKE

98. **Jumbles:** PANDA MINOR DONKEY FIERCE
**Answer:** "Where can you buy camel's milk?"—AT A "DROME-DAIRY"

99. **Jumbles:** QUEST GAWKY DENOTE SURELY
**Answer:** What to wear when working outdoors—A "LAWN DRESS"

100. **Jumbles:** POUND BOUGH FERVID TALKER
**Answer:** What caused the puncture in the tire?—A FORK IN THE ROAD

101. **Jumbles:** POKED HONOR GULLET FAMISH
**Answer:** What a visitor to Hawaii is interested in finding out about first—THE "LEI" OF THE LAND

102. **Jumbles:** WEIGH GNARL BANDIT FICKLE
**Answer:** Whether it rained or not the weather caster was this most of the time—ALL WET

103. **Jumbles:** FAULT BROIL FLABBY MEASLY
**Answer:** When is a boat the cheapest?—WHEN IT'S A "SALE" BOAT

104. **Jumbles:** TRACT ACRID CONVEX BUBBLE
**Answer:** What the India rubber man at the circus got—BOUNCED

105. **Jumbles:** AGONY ENACT BUCKLE NICELY
**Answer:** What her companions called that stupid hen—A BIG CLUCK

106. **Jumbles:** FAITH PROXY GLOBAL EYEFUL
**Answer:** Why the cop turned musician got fired from the band—HE WAS "OFF BEAT"

107. **Jumbles:** SOGGY TAKEN CENSUS BROGUE
**Answer:** What you'd expect to have for breakfast at a lighthouse—"BEACON" & EGGS

108. **Jumbles:** KNELL TABOO PUZZLE MEMBER
**Answer:** What sailing a boat on a nice windy day can be—A BREEZE

109. **Jumbles:** FLUID SURLY INJURY BEHEAD
**Answer:** A stern necessity on a boat—A RUDDER

110. **Jumbles:** QUEEN BELLE BISHOP MAGPIE
**Answer:** A fisherman sometimes stands still while fishing, but more often does this—LIES

111. **Jumbles:** NAVAL TASTY STIGMA RADIUS
**Answer:** The regatta was so full of sailboats that it made one think of this—"MAST" TRANSIT

112. **Jumbles:** INKED LUCID CASHEW DIVERT
**Answer:** What those tourists got while in Holland—IN DUTCH

113. **Jumbles:** IDIOT BERTH POLISH AMBUSH
**Answer:** When neighbors gossip over a fence, there's much to be said—ON BOTH SIDES

114. **Jumbles:** ARDOR RIVET FUNGUS EFFORT
**Answer:** What it takes for a deadbeat to keep afloat—A RAFT OF FRIENDS

115. **Jumbles:** VYING DEMON RATIFY TREATY
**Answer:** That spoiled kid would rather cry and get it than—TRY AND GET IT

116. **Jumbles:** ELEGY PANIC BOUNCE FABRIC
**Answer:** Another name for all that baggage that goes into the vehicle—"CAR-GO"

117. **Jumbles:** TEMPO BLOOD MARVEL EMPIRE
**Answer:** What a skilled gardener knows how to do—IMPROVE HIS "LOT"

118. **Jumbles:** ENACT JUICY CONCUR TIPTOE
**Answer:** What a picnic with kids sometimes is—"NO PICNIC"

119. **Jumbles:** BAKED AFOOT RADIUM VERMIN
**Answer:** What the sailor shouted when he saw the surfer—MAN "OVER BOARD"

120. **Jumbles:** ABATE PIKER TURTLE LOCATE
**Answer:** If you're concerned about rattlesnakes, start running when you hear this—A TATTLE "TAIL"

121. **Jumbles:** BERET NAIVE MAGNET SCHOOL
**Answer:** What the lion tamer would have preferred—TAMER LIONS

122. **Jumbles:** NOISY CABIN SADIST HEARSE
**Answer:** For a mother—THE SON ALWAYS SHINES

123. **Jumbles:** HELLO CRANK ENTITY WEASEL
**Answer:** In her bathing suit, she revealed legs that were this—"SEEWORTHY"

124. **Jumbles:** GLOVE CRAZY EXTANT RANCOR
**Answer:** There are some who say this is the best butter—A GOAT

125. **Jumbles:** CRIME QUAIL BECKON HECTIC
**Answer:** Never have so many owed so much to so little—THE BIKINI

126. **Jumbles:** TOXIN BELIE DEADLY TUMULT
**Answer:** The moon affects this—THE TIDE AND THE UNTIED

127. **Jumbles:** FLAKE MAXIM VANITY HANGAR
**Answer:** In politics this is where the "paths of glory" might lead—TO THE "GRAVY"

128. **Jumbles:** POWER GUILE FONDLY SQUIRM
**Answer:** The hardest thing to raise in a garden—YOURSELF

129. **Jumbles:** ROBIN BYLAW VELVET CENSUS
**Answer:** A leash is a line by which a dog is held in check by a person—OR VICE VERSA

130. **Jumbles:** TAKEN POUCH SURTAX HOPPER
**Answer:** What a bathing suit develops after it's put on—A SHAPE

131. **Jumbles:** PEACE OLDER DEFAME GRATIS
**Answer:** Will a college education help him to succeed in life?—TO SOME "DEGREE"

132. **Jumbles:** RIGOR ABHOR BRIDLE INTAKE
**Answer:** What they called that daft ornithologist—"BIRDBRAIN"

133. **Jumbles:** ELEGY LIMBO MISUSE TAMPER
**Answer:** Could be the good old summertime—"SIMMER TIME"

134. **Jumbles:** YIELD GLORY TINKLE UNHOLY
**Answer:** A bachelor is a man who can go fishing anytime—UNTIL HE GETS "HOOKED"

135. **Jumbles:** HURRY FOLIO CANNED TEACUP
**Answer:** The gardener found that topsoil is no longer this—"DIRT" CHEAP

136. **Jumbles:** CHAOS PLAID BASKET MARAUD
**Answer:** It was so hot, the thermometer was this—UP IN THE "HADES"

137. **Jumbles:** DROOP COACH BLEACH RECTOR
**Answer:** What the bird was looking for when he flew over all those fish—A "PERCH"

138. **Jumbles:** FLUID HAVEN MUSCLE EXCITE
**Answer:** Why the contortionist combed his hair with his toes—TO MAKE ENDS MEET

139. **Jumbles:** RUSTY FEVER ZODIAC ENZYME
**Answer:** Where that eccentric dancer went—CRAZY WITH THE "FEET"

140. **Jumbles:** PANDA LEAKY CHORUS FUTILE
**Answer:** These words came to mind when he saw that glider pilot—"SOAR" "FEAT"

141. **Jumbles:** LANKY COUPE DECENT NOVICE
**Answer:** Another thing a young mother should save for a rainy day—PATIENCE

142. **Jumbles:** LOONY MOLDY CABANA KETTLE
**Answer:** Where can you find a good card game on a big ship?—ANY "DECK"

143. **Jumbles:** BRAND FUROR DETACH SALUTE
**Answer:** What the farmer had that made the cow jump over the moon—COLD HANDS

144. **Jumbles:** JUICE HASTY TYPIST NICETY
**Answer:** What they expected the ballplayer to do when he joined their camping party—"PITCH" THE TENT

145. **Jumbles:** ENVOY DIZZY MILDEW SICKEN
**Answer:** The only people who were safe when that man-eating tiger got loose—WOMEN & KIDS

146. **Jumbles:** HONEY GUIDE SPLICE POSTAL
**Answer:** Responsible for the holdup in the back yard—CLOTHESPINS

147. **Jumbles:** POWER NOVEL GENTRY TANDEM
**Answer:** Their family pet was so bright that he earned this—HIS "DOG-TORATE"

148. **Jumbles:** ABHOR BLOOD HUMBLE TRYING
**Answer:** "Your family wash in the backyard?"—"NO, IN THE BATHROOM"

149. **Jumbles:** ANKLE CARGO PEWTER ANGINA
**Answer:** How the fishing fleet caught its daily limit—BY "NET"-WORKING

150. **Jumbles:** AMUSE DECRY HECKLE HYBRID
**Answer:** What the guard did to the ship's intruder—HE DECKED HIM

151. **Jumbles:** AVAIL FANCY DOUBLE TACKLE
**Answer:** The tightrope walker got into trouble because he had a—LACK OF BALANCE

152. **Jumbles:** IDIOT BASIN CORPSE NIBBLE
**Answer:** How the visitors reacted to the sponge diver's lecture—THEY WERE ABSORBED

153. **Jumbles:** NEWLY SMOKY CRAVAT GUITAR
**Answer:** What they became when the insects attacked—THE SWAT TEAM

154. **Jumbles:** HAVOC ELDER ARTERY HUMBLE
**Answer:** The kind of life some snakes lead—CHARMED

155. **Jumbles:** FLAKE ELEGY CORRAL RITUAL
**Answer:** What the birds gave the nature lovers—A REAL TRILL

156. **Jumbles:** TARDY IVORY ANKLET TIMELY
**Answer:** What some leave behind when getting away from it all—VERY LITTLE

157. **Jumbles:** TRILL EXUDE AFRAID BODILY
**Answer:** What the landscaper uncovered in the royal garden—THE REAL DIRT

158. **Jumbles:** CABIN CLOUT COERCE DISMAY
**Answer:** Why the bank robbers headed for the seashore—THE COAST WAS CLEAR

159. **Jumbles:** PENCE MAGIC BUSILY FIERCE
**Answer:** What he offered the prospective buyer—A "SAIL" PRICE

160. **Jumbles:** CRESS POWER FARINA COUGAR
**Answer:** Why the pilot couldn't decide where to land—HE WAS UP IN THE AIR

161. **Jumbles:** GUILE AFTER SUBDUE GIGGLE
**Answer:** How she improved her knowledge—BY DEGREES

162. **Jumbles:** NOTCH OUNCE UPKEEP COOKIE
**Answer:** What the poultry farmer called the car he drove to market—HIS CHICKEN COUPE

163. **Jumbles:** GAUGE ANISE GOATEE NETHER
**Answer:** How the chicken farmer got his start—WITH A NEST EGG

164. **Jumbles:** AGLOW FRUIT BYGONE SCRIBE
**Answer:** What he did when she forgot the sun block lotion—A SLOW BURN

165. **Jumbles:** NAIVE NATAL DAHLIA KOSHER
**Answer:** What the phone operator liked to do on vacation—HOLD THE LINE

166. **Jumbles:** ALTAR FLUID MUSEUM WHEEZE
**Answer:** What the well-to-do candy maker enjoyed—THE SWEET LIFE

167. **Jumbles:** ABBEY CROAK CHROME HOTBED
**Answer:** What the hair stylist at the seashore was called—A BEACH COMBER

168. **Jumbles:** MOSAIC CLOVEN ZIGZAG JUGGLE VICUNA QUAVER
**Answer:** Why modern swimsuits are real "cool"—THEY'RE REAL "GONE"

169. **Jumbles:** CAVIAR UNPACK BEFALL MAKEUP EXCISE QUAINT
**Answer:** What you get on this farm—QUACKERS & MILK

170. **Jumbles:** IMPUTE COUPON EXOTIC BOYISH RADIUS STOLID
**Answer:** What you'll find plenty of at the beach on Sunday—COMIC STRIPS

171. **Jumbles:** PRISON TRIPLE SALUTE INVOKE MOTIVE ALIGHT
**Answer:** How to get your clothes off faster than the others—OUTSTRIP THEM

172. **Jumbles:** TURTLE PONCHO GUNNER ESTATE INWARD UNSAID
**Answer:** What happened when the grapes were trampled on—THEY LET OUT A "WINE"

173. **Jumbles:** DETAIN ICEBOX FORAGE BARREL CLOTHE HANDLE
**Answer:** What he said when asked why he stole a purse—I NEEDED THE CHANGE

174. **Jumbles:** BRANDY DAMAGE SPLICE CLOUDY INFANT SWIVEL
**Answer:** What he hoped the hula dancer would be—EASILY SWAYED

175. **Jumbles:** IMPACT SOOTHE ACTUAL OUTWIT HANGER WOEFUL
**Answer:** A see-through shirt might be suitable for a man who has to do this—WATCH HIS WAISTLINE

176. **Jumbles:** DOMINO OUTLAW INWARD USEFUL MIDDAY AFFRAY
**Answer:** What a sheepskin is intended to keep—THE WOLF AWAY FROM THE DOOR

177. **Jumbles:** TINKLE DAMAGE HICCUP ADRIFT MORGUE POISON
**Answer:** What you might end up with if you happen to touch poison ivy while picking a four-leaf clover—A "RASH" OF GOOD LUCK

178. **Jumbles:** MISERY PILFER ASSURE WHENCE THIRTY STANZA
**Answer:** What an oldster sometimes prefers—A SIESTA TO FIESTA

179. **Jumbles:** CHARGE FALLOW GRUBBY ZODIAC ROSARY ANKLET
**Answer:** What kind of a character was the guy who was lying under a tree watching his wife mow the lawn?—A SHADY ONE

180. **Jumbles:** ANYHOW BAKING TANKER JOCUND INDUCE FALTER
**Answer:** Why the apprentice trapeze artist couldn't hold the job—HE DIDN'T CATCH ON

188

# Need More Jumbles®?

Order any of these books through your bookseller or call Triumph Books toll-free at 800-335-5323.

## Jumble® Books

**More than 175 puzzles each!**

**Cowboy Jumble®**
ISBN: 978-1-62937-355-3

**Jammin' Jumble®**
ISBN: 1-57243-844-4

**Java Jumble®**
ISBN: 978-1-60078-415-6

**Jazzy Jumble®**
ISBN: 978-1-57243-962-7

**Jet Set Jumble®**
ISBN: 978-1-60078-353-1

**Joyful Jumble®**
ISBN: 978-1-60078-079-0

**Juke Joint Jumble®**
ISBN: 978-1-60078-295-4

**Jumble® Anniversary**
ISBN: 987-1-62937-734-6

**Jumble® at Work**
ISBN: 1-57243-147-4

**Jumble® Ballet**
ISBN: 978-1-62937-616-5

**Jumble® Birthday**
ISBN: 978-1-62937-652-3

**Jumble® Celebration**
ISBN: 978-1-60078-134-6

**Jumble® Circus**
ISBN: 978-1-60078-739-3

**Jumble® Cuisine**
ISBN: 978-1-62937-735-3

**Jumble® Drag Race**
ISBN: 978-1-62937-483-3

**Jumble® Ever After**
ISBN: 978-1-62937-785-8

**Jumble® Explorer**
ISBN: 978-1-60078-854-3

**Jumble® Explosion**
ISBN: 978-1-60078-078-3

**Jumble® Fever**
ISBN: 1-57243-593-3

**Jumble® Fiesta**
ISBN: 1-57243-626-3

**Jumble® Fun**
ISBN: 1-57243-379-5

**Jumble® Galaxy**
ISBN: 978-1-60078-583-2

**Jumble® Garden**
ISBN: 978-1-62937-653-0

**Jumble® Genius**
ISBN: 1-57243-896-7

**Jumble® Geography**
ISBN: 978-1-62937-615-8

**Jumble® Getaway**
ISBN: 978-1-60078-547-4

**Jumble® Gold**
ISBN: 978-1-62937-354-6

**Jumble® Grab Bag**
ISBN: 1-57243-273-X

**Jumble® Gymnastics**
ISBN: 978-1-62937-306-5

**Jumble® Jackpot**
ISBN: 1-57243-897-5

**Jumble® Jailbreak**
ISBN: 978-1-62937-002-6

**Jumble® Jambalaya**
ISBN: 978-1-60078-294-7

**Jumble® Jamboree**
ISBN: 1-57243-696-4

**Jumble® Jitterbug**
ISBN: 978-1-60078-584-9

**Jumble® Journey**
ISBN: 978-1-62937-549-6

**Jumble® Jubilation**
ISBN: 978-1-62937-784-1

**Jumble® Jubilee**
ISBN: 1-57243-231-4

**Jumble® Juggernaut**
ISBN: 978-1-60078-026-4

**Jumble® Junction**
ISBN: 1-57243-380-9

**Jumble® Jungle**
ISBN: 978-1-57243-961-0

**Jumble® Kingdom**
ISBN: 978-1-62937-079-8

**Jumble® Knockout**
ISBN: 978-1-62937-078-1

**Jumble® Madness**
ISBN: 1-892049-24-4

**Jumble® Magic**
ISBN: 978-1-60078-795-9

**Jumble® Marathon**
ISBN: 978-1-60078-944-1

**Jumble® Neighbor**
ISBN: 978-1-62937-845-9

**Jumble® Parachute**
ISBN: 978-1-62937-548-9

**Jumble® Safari**
ISBN: 978-1-60078-675-4

**Jumble® See & Search**
ISBN: 1-57243-549-6

**Jumble® See & Search 2**
ISBN: 1-57243-734-0

**Jumble® Sensation**
ISBN: 978-1-60078-548-1

**Jumble® Surprise**
ISBN: 1-57243-320-5

**Jumble® Symphony**
ISBN: 978-1-62937-131-3

**Jumble® Theater**
ISBN: 978-1-62937-484-03

**Jumble® University**
ISBN: 978-1-62937-001-9

**Jumble® Unleashed**
ISBN: 978-1-62937-844-2

**Jumble® Vacation**
ISBN: 978-1-60078-796-6

**Jumble® Wedding**
ISBN: 978-1-62937-307-2

**Jumble® Workout**
ISBN: 978-1-60078-943-4

**Jumpin' Jumble®**
ISBN: 978-1-60078-027-1

**Lunar Jumble®**
ISBN: 978-1-60078-853-6

**Monster Jumble®**
ISBN: 978-1-62937-213-6

**Mystic Jumble®**
ISBN: 978-1-62937-130-6

**Outer Space Jumble®**
ISBN: 978-1-60078-416-3

**Rainy Day Jumble®**
ISBN: 978-1-60078-352-4

**Ready, Set, Jumble®**
ISBN: 978-1-60078-133-0

**Rock 'n' Roll Jumble®**
ISBN: 978-1-60078-674-7

**Royal Jumble®**
ISBN: 978-1-60078-738-6

**Sports Jumble®**
ISBN: 1-57243-113-X

**Summer Fun Jumble®**
ISBN: 1-57243-114-8

**Touchdown Jumble®**
ISBN: 978-1-62937-212-9

**Travel Jumble®**
ISBN: 1-57243-198-9

**TV Jumble®**
ISBN: 1-57243-461-9

## Oversize Jumble® Books

**More than 500 puzzles each!**

**Generous Jumble®**
ISBN: 1-57243-385-X

**Giant Jumble®**
ISBN: 1-57243-349-3

**Gigantic Jumble®**
ISBN: 1-57243-426-0

**Jumbo Jumble®**
ISBN: 1-57243-314-0

**The Very Best of Jumble® BrainBusters**
ISBN: 1-57243-845-2

## Jumble® Crosswords™

**More than 175 puzzles each!**

**More Jumble® Crosswords™**
ISBN: 1-57243-386-8

**Jumble® Crosswords™ Jackpot**
ISBN: 1-57243-615-8

**Jumble® Crosswords™ Jamboree**
ISBN: 1-57243-787-1

## Jumble® BrainBusters™

**More than 175 puzzles each!**

**Jumble® BrainBusters™**
ISBN: 1-892049-28-7

**Jumble® BrainBusters™ II**
ISBN: 1-57243-424-4

**Jumble® BrainBusters™ III**
ISBN: 1-57243-463-5

**Jumble® BrainBusters™ IV**
ISBN: 1-57243-489-9

**Jumble® BrainBusters™ 5**
ISBN: 1-57243-548-8

**Jumble® BrainBusters™ Bonanza**
ISBN: 1-57243-616-6

**Boggle™ BrainBusters™**
ISBN: 1-57243-592-5

**Boggle™ BrainBusters™ 2**
ISBN: 1-57243-788-X

**Jumble® BrainBusters™ Junior**
ISBN: 1-892049-29-5

**Jumble® BrainBusters™ Junior II**
ISBN: 1-57243-425-2

**Fun in the Sun with Jumble® BrainBusters™**
ISBN: 1-57243-733-2